True Worship

'Highly commended for all thinking Christians who want to be the kind of worshippers the Father seeks, worshipping "in Spirit and in Truth".'

Evangelicals Now

True Worship

Vaughan Roberts

Authentic

First published in 2002 by Authentic Lifestyle

23 22 21 20 19 18   15 14 13 12 11 10

Reprinted in 2012, 2016 and 2018 by Authentic Media Limited
Po Box 6326, Bletchley, Milton, Keynes MK1 9GG
www.authenticmedia.co.uk

British Library Cataloguing in Publication Data
A catalogue record for this book is available from the British
Library.

ISBN 978-1-85078-445-6

Cover Design by David McNeill (www.revocreative.co.uk).
Printed and bound by CPI Group (UK) Ltd., Croydon, CR0 4YY.

**To the church family at
St Ebbe's**
Philippians 1:3–6

Contents

Acknowledgements   ix

Introduction   xi

1 The Foundations of Christian Worship
'In Spirit and in Truth'   1

2 The Nature of Christian Worship
'Living Sacrifices'   14

3 The End of Religion
'He sat down'   27

4 The Purpose of Christian Meetings
'Encourage one another'   43

5 The Place of Music and Singing
'Sing and make music in your heart to the Lord'   65

6 Understanding the Lord's Supper
'Do this in remembrance of me'   85

Appendix:
Christ's Sacrifice and Ours   102

Acknowledgements

I am grateful to Clare Heath-Whyte, Matthew Mason, Mark Thompson and Andy Virr for commenting on the manuscript and to Liz Chang and Glenn B. Nesbitt for their typing.

Introduction

Have you noticed how often religious terminology is used in connection with sport? The newspapers were full of it during a recent Olympic Games. I read that Jonathan Edwards had at last 'found the Holy Grail' when he won the Triple Jump Gold Medal. Cathy Freeman 'joined the pantheon of Olympic gods and the stadium was referred to as 'the Mecca of world sport'.

An advert for a satellite television station announced a football match that was going to be broadcast live. Underneath a picture of a television screen was this message: 'Worship here this Wednesday.' A poster announcing the arrival of the new Volkswagen Golf had a similar theme. An arrow pointed to the driver's seat, and next to it were those words again: 'Worship here'.

Most of us sense that the language of worship is inappropriate when applied to sport or cars. God alone is worthy of worship. But what does that actually mean? 'Worship' is a slippery word. We use it often and we think we understand it, but we find it very hard to define. What does it mean to worship God, and how should we do it? The Buddhist monk with his prayer wheel, the Roman Catholic nun with her rosary and the

Muslim bowing down in prayer at the mosque all think they are worshipping God. But are they? People ask us: "Where do you worship?' by which they mean: 'Where do you go to church?' Others leave a Christian meeting and say: 'It was a great time of worship tonight', by which they mean the singing. Is that all that worship is? Church on a Sunday or, more specifically, a time of singing in church on Sunday? Or is there more to it than that? What is worship? And how should we do it?

Those are vital questions. The Lord Jesus referred to 'true worshippers' who are 'the kind of worshippers the Father seeks'.[1] The implication is clear: there is such a thing as false worship that does not please God. Just think about that for a moment. It would be a dreadful thing to be deluded in this matter – to think we are pleasing God, and that we are worshipping him, when we are not. The only way to avoid that mistake is to find out what God wants by turning to his word, the Bible. That is what we will be doing in this short book. I have written it because I am concerned that much of our thinking about worship is confused and often unbiblical. Do not take my word for it; make up your own mind as you study the Scriptures to see what God says about this important subject.

---

[1] Jn. 4:23.

1

The Foundations of Christian Worship
'In Spirit and in Truth'

[19]'Sir,' the woman said, 'I can see that you are a prophet. [20]Our fathers worshipped on this mountain, but you Jews claim that the place where we must worship is in Jerusalem.'
[21]Jesus declared, 'Believe me, woman, a time is coming when you will worship the Father neither on this mountain nor in Jerusalem. [22]You Samaritans worship what you do not know; we worship what we do know, for salvation is from the Jews. [23]Yet a time is coming and has now come when the true worshippers will worship the Father in spirit and truth, for they are the kind of worshippers the Father seeks. [24]God is spirit, and his worshippers must worship in spirit and in truth' (Jn. 4:19-24).

I love the account of this encounter between Jesus and the Samaritan woman in the fourth chapter of John's gospel. It is remarkable that the conversation took place at all. Jewish men would not normally have been seen talking to women in public, let alone Samaritan women.

Jews despised Samaritans as racial mongrels and religious heretics. And, what is more, this particular woman was known for her loose living (vv. 16-18). Most people would have shunned her, but Jesus was never bound by social conventions. He reached out to everyone. He spoke to this woman with great tenderness and compassion. Their conversation turned to the subject of worship and points to three things without which we will not be able truly to worship God:

> The Lord Jesus himself
> The Holy Spirit
> The truth

A. True worship is impossible without Jesus Christ

Jesus offers the Samaritan woman 'living water' (v. 10). At first, she misses the point: she thinks he is talking about literal water. But when he reveals a supernatural knowledge about her (he is aware of her multiple marriages), she begins to realize that she is talking to someone really special: 'Sir, I can see that you are a prophet' (v. 19). What she says next is strange to our ears: 'Our fathers worshipped on this mountain, but you Jews claim that the place where we must worship is in Jerusalem' (v. 20).

Some commentators have accused her of introducing a red herring into the conversation. They suggest that she feels the spiritual heat rising and so brings up this safe theological topic for discussion, to direct the focus away from herself and her immoral life. I doubt that. The issue she raises was of great importance at the time. It concerned the question of true worship. Where should people go if they wanted to meet with God?

Should they go to Mount Gerizim, as the Samaritans believed (that was where their temple was), or to Jerusalem, as the Jews believed? Who was right? It is still an important question today. Where can God be found?

Where can God be found?

Someone begins to seek after truth. Where should they go? To Mecca or Jerusalem? To the Bible or the Baghavad Gita? To Jesus or Buddha? Where can God be found? It is a vital question. We will never be able to worship God rightly until we find the answer. The subject this woman raises is not a smokescreen to avoid the real issue. No, this is the real issue. Perhaps what Jesus has said has awakened a genuine spiritual interest in her heart – she wants to meet with God. But where should she go to find him?

Jesus' reply is not what she expected: 'Believe me, woman, a time is coming when you will worship the Father neither on this mountain [Gerizim] nor in Jerusalem' (v. 21). He is saying that it will not be long before the ancient dispute between those two great temples will be obsolete. She will not have to go to either place for a genuine encounter with the living God. He is not ducking the question. He makes it clear just where he stands on this disputed issue: 'You Samaritans worship what you do not know; we worship what we do know, for salvation is from the Jews' (v. 22). The Samaritans were wrong and the Jews were right. God did choose to focus his presence with his people in the temple in Jerusalem, not Gerizim. For centuries Jerusalem had been the place to which he expected his people to come to meet with him. But all that was about to change: 'Yet a time is coming and has now come when the true worshippers will worship the Father in spirit and truth' (v. 23). A new way of engaging with God was about to be introduced. It would not depend on any one place. It would depend on 'spirit and truth'.

There are no more holy places

That is radical teaching. All over the world, people and religions have set apart special places and designated them 'holy'. In their understanding, if you want to meet with God you have to go to a shrine, a temple, a mosque, or a church. When I was travelling in Israel a few years ago, I managed to get barred from both a mosque and a church on the same day. I was told that shorts were not suitable attire. I asked what the problem was. The reply came: 'This is God's house.' Apparently the Almighty would be shocked at the sight of my knees.

Some people bow towards the front on entering a church building, as if somehow God lived up there. They would be horrified if they knew that we serve hot dogs from the chancel after the Sunday evening meeting at our church in Oxford. But there is in fact nothing inappropriate about that. We must not think of a church building as 'the house of God'. There are no holy places any more. For generations, you had to go to the temple at Jerusalem if you wanted to meet with God. But he had never intended that to continue forever. Through the prophets, he spoke of a new age in the future when everything would change. That new age would be introduced when the Messiah, God's Son, came to earth.

Jesus changes everything

The Samaritan woman knew enough theology to realize that, so she said: 'I know that Messiah is coming. When he comes, he will explain everything to us' (v. 25). And Jesus tells her that he has come: 'I who speak to you am he' (v. 26). God has come to earth in the person of his son, the Lord Jesus Christ, and that changes everything. In the past people had to go to the temple in Jerusalem for a genuine encounter with God: that is where he focused his revelation of himself. But all that changes once the Messiah comes. True worship is dependent now on a person, not a place; on Jesus, not the temple. He is the fulfilment of all that went before. The time has come because Jesus has come.

Chartwell was Winston Churchill's private house. It is open to the public and displays a whole range of items that belonged to him – some of his clothes, a few letters and the odd cigar. As you look at them, you can almost get a sense of the presence of the great man. But just imagine that Winston Churchill could somehow come back to life and you heard he was living in London. You would not go to Chartwell any more if you wanted to be close to him and get to know him; you would go to London. There would be no point in going to see a few cigars that are merely symbols of his presence; you would go see the man himself. In a similar way, the temple is made redundant once Jesus comes. It contained only symbols of God's presence, tablets of stone with his commandments, pointing to his holy character. But with Jesus comes more than a symbol; he is the reality itself, God himself in human form. So if we want to meet with God and worship him, we do not have to go to any special place – be it Gerizim, or Jerusalem, or a church building. We must come instead to a special person, the Lord Jesus. He rose from the dead and is alive today, and through him we are able to enter into a direct and personal relationship with the true and living God.

Do you want to worship God? You do not have to go to a religious building or place. You must come to Jesus. True worship is impossible without Jesus Christ. The next two points we will consider, that we also need the Holy Spirit and the truth, are really only extensions of this fundamental truth.

B. True worship is impossible without the Holy Spirit

Jesus said: 'God is spirit, and his worshippers must worship in spirit and in truth' (v. 24). There has been some debate as to what exactly Jesus means by 'spirit'. Some have argued that he is referring to the human spirit, 'the inner me'. If this is the case, he is saying that true worship is not about externals – special rituals in holy buildings. It begins, rather, in the heart; it must be an internal reality, in my spirit. That is undoubtedly true, but I think Jesus is saying much more than that here. 'Spirit' refers to the Holy Spirit. There can be no true worship without him. In other words, true worship is supernatural. It is not something I can offer by myself. I need God's help, by his Spirit, to worship him properly.

We have seen already that if I want to worship God I need to come to Jesus, God's Son – I will only find God through Jesus. The true worshipper is the one who recognizes Jesus for who he is, the living God, and then seeks to live accordingly. The nature of Christian worship is the theme of Chapter 2, but we are bound to touch on it here. Worship cannot be limited to what we do in church on Sunday. Worship means submitting to Jesus Christ in every area of my life, and that is something I cannot do by myself; it is impossible for me because it clashes with my natural desire to live to please myself rather than the God who made me.

Self-worship

By nature, I worship myself. I live as if I am God. I live for my desires, my comforts, my ambitions. That is what we are all like by nature. But Jesus calls us to change. He demands that we dethrone ourselves and live instead for him as our king. He commands us to throw our own crowns at his feet and start living lives of submission and obedience to him. That is what it takes to be a true worshipper and, by myself, I cannot do it. It is fairly easy to turn up at church on a Sunday, say some prayers and sing a few songs. Anyone can say, 'I believe in God; Father, Son and Holy Spirit'. Anyone can sing: "I love you Lord and I lift my voice to worship you.' But true worship means more than that. It is not just words, but actions as well, for I show what I really think about Jesus by the way that I live. To truly worship, I need to change the whole direction of my life. Worship means showing my love for Christ by living for him in my family, among my friends, at work or college, at the party or in the car. And that is something I cannot do by myself; it is impossible for me.

There is a terrible indictment of human beings in the previous chapter of John's Gospel: 'This is the verdict: Light has come into the world, but men loved darkness instead of light because their deeds were evil' (Jn. 3:19). When the Lord Jesus Christ came into the world, people did not bow down and worship him, as they should have done. Instead, they ran away from him. We do not like the light. We are like those little insects in the dirt that run for cover when you lift up a brick or a stone. Jesus is a threat to our much-prized independence. He challenges our lifestyle. We know that if we start worshipping him, that worship cannot be contained in a little building on a Sunday. It is bound to have repercussions for every part of our lives and we do not like the sound of that. By nature we worship ourselves.

'You must be born again'

So how can true worship be possible? It is all very well to say that we can only worship God through Jesus Christ, but how will I ever come to Jesus Christ, if by nature I run away from him? The answer is that I will only come to Jesus by the Spirit. It takes a miracle of God to make a worshipper. That was even true for Nicodemus, a very religious man whose meeting with Jesus is recorded in John 3. He thought he had been worshipping God all his life, but he had not been. Jesus tells him: 'I tell you the truth, no-one can see the kingdom of God unless he is born again' (v. 3).

No one can become a friend of God, no one can become a true worshipper, by his own goodness, her own efforts, his religion. Our only hope is if we become completely new people. We must be born again. Nicodemus knows that is impossible for him: 'How can a man be born when he is old? ... Surely he cannot enter a second time into his mother's womb to be born!' (v. 4) But what is impossible for us is possible with God, through the intervention of God's Spirit. Jesus said: 'I tell you the truth, no-one can enter the kingdom of God unless he is born of water and the Spirit' (v. 5). We need to be born again. We need a miracle if we are ever going to bow down at Jesus' feet and become true worshippers of God. Because that miracle comes only through the Holy Spirit, true worshippers must worship 'in Spirit'.

'Worship in Spirit' does not, therefore, refer to speaking in tongues or exercising other particular spiritual gifts. Nor is Jesus referring to emotional times of singing. This worship is not the preserve of only a select band of Christians. All those who are born again 'worship in Spirit' – the one leads to the other. To 'worship in Spirit' is to acknowledge Jesus as God and live accordingly. It is conversion and the life that flows out of it. John's Gospel never divides the work of Jesus and the work of the Spirit; they belong together. It is the Spirit who brings us to Jesus and enables us to worship God in the first place and then empowers us to continue doing so. True worship is impossible without the Spirit.

It may be that you have been going to church for years. You have been baptized and received the Lord's Supper often. You are in the church choir or music group and love to sing Christian songs. But it is still possible that you have never begun to worship God. I went to over 2,500 Christian meetings before I was born again. Only then did the Spirit intervene in my life and draw me to Jesus Christ. Do not confuse religion with true worship. Have you come to Christ, put your trust in him and begun to live for him? If not, pray that God would work that miracle in your life and give you the new birth of which Jesus spoke. Pray that he would make you a true worshipper.

C. True worship is impossible without the truth

Some readers may be thinking: 'I can accept that it's a good thing to worship God through Jesus Christ. I don't have a problem with that, but surely, there must be other ways as well? Think of all the people in the world, worshipping God so sincerely. You're not really saying, are you, that true worship is something that only Christians can offer?' Yes, I am saying exactly that, because that is what Jesus taught.

We cannot pick and choose how we worship. We must worship 'in spirit *and in truth*'. Truth is not a popular concept these days. We live in a pluralistic society. People around us believe in all sorts of different things, and we are considered highly arrogant and offensive if we claim that we have the truth and that those who disagree with us are wrong. Shirley Maclean, the actress and New Age guru, said once: 'Everyone has his own truth and truth as an objective reality does not exist.' But Jesus would not agree. He refers not just to *a* truth or to subjective truth, but to *the* truth – there is no other. He famously said: 'I am the way and the truth and the life. No-one comes to the Father except through me' (Jn. 14:6). He is not just one option among many. He is unique; he alone makes true worship possible.

Jesus is the truth

Jesus alone is the perfect revelation of God. He makes true worship possible because he shows us what God is really like. We are not to blindly worship a god that we have imagined. We are to worship the one true God, who makes himself known to us through Jesus, his one and only son. Other religions begin on earth, with human beings looking up into an unseen heaven and speculating as to what God might be like. But Christianity is not based on speculation. It begins in heaven, with God taking the initiative to come to earth to reveal truth to us about himself. Because we have this truth, we are able to worship God as he really is, not simply as we imagine him to be.

But we need more than revelation to make true worship possible. It is not just ignorance that prevents us from worshipping God: our sin does as well. By nature, we turn away from God. As a result, we are under his judgement, cut off from him. We need not only revelation, but redemption as well. We need to be brought back into relationship with him. And Jesus is the redeemer, the rescuer, we need. He offers perfect revelation and he also achieved a perfect redemption.

The crucial 'hour'

Twice in his conversation with the Samaritan woman Jesus tells her that 'a time is coming'. He speaks of a future moment when everything will change. From then on, places will not matter, neither Gerizim nor Jerusalem. 'A time is coming,' he says, when 'true worshippers will worship ... in spirit and truth' (v. 23). A more literal translation of his phrase is: 'the hour is coming'. Jesus speaks of 'the hour' on a number of occasions in John's Gospel. 'The hour' had a very special significance for him, for it was the decisive moment when the new age would be introduced. It refers to his death and what follows it – his resurrection and ascension into heaven.[1] It is 'the hour' that makes true worship possible. His death changes everything.

On the cross Jesus dealt with the great barrier that cuts us off from his Father, by taking the punishment for our wrongdoing upon himself. As a result, he makes it possible for us all to enter God's presence and live life in friendship with him. He died to make us worshippers. By nature, I worship myself. Jesus Christ took on himself the punishment for my self-worship and self-glorification. He thus made it possible for me to come back into friendship with God. I am now free to become a worshipper again.

A.W. Tozer put it like this:

---

[1] Jn. 2:4; 7:30; 8:20; 12:23,27; 13:1; 17:1.

The purpose of God in sending his son to die and rise
and live and be at the right hand of God the Father was
that he might restore to us the missing jewel, the jewel of
worship; that we might come back and learn to do again
that which we were created to do in the first place – worship the Lord in the beauty of holiness, to spend our time
in awesome wonder and adoration of God, feeling it and
expressing it, and letting it get into our labours, and
doing nothing except as an act of worship to Almighty
God through his son Jesus Christ.[2]

The saving work of Christ makes worship possible. He
alone is the truth; there is no other way to God. He provides the revelation and redemption, without which
true worship is impossible. So, if I am to worship as I
should, I need to hear the truth about Jesus. That truth is
not found anywhere except within the gospel of Christ,
proclaimed in the Bible.

I assume you are already a follower of Christ and are
trying to live a life of worship. That began when God
enabled you to understand the truth about Jesus and
respond to it with faith and repentance. If we are to continue to worship him properly we need to keep hearing
the truth about him. Worship never begins with us; it is
always a response to the truth. It flows out of an understanding of who God is and what he has done for us in
Christ. It begins with his revelation and redemption. So
we must ensure that the Bible, which contains that revelation and points us to God's work of redemption, stays
right at the heart of our meetings and our own spiritual
lives. Prior to speaking at different meetings I have
received letters which tell me: 'Keep the talk short

---

[2] A.W. Tozer, *The Missing Jewel of the Evangelical Church*
(Harrisburg, PA: Christian Publications, n.d.), 12.

because we want as much time as possible for worshipping God.' But how can I worship God properly without being reminded of the truth? It is God's truth in the Bible that fuels my worship of him throughout the week.

Three in one

True worship is impossible without Jesus Christ, the Holy Spirit and the truth. Do you see how those three points really merge into one? True worship is only possible through Jesus, because of his unique revelation and redemption. But we cannot respond to him unless we hear about who he is and what he has done – we need the truth. But even that is not enough, because I will never respond to the truth without the help of the Holy Spirit, who is referred to in John's Gospel as 'the Spirit of truth'.[3] We must not divide the Spirit from the truth and refer to anything emotional (for instance a time of singing) as the Spirit's work, and refer to anything cerebral (such as a Bible study) as the truth at work. No, God the Spirit uses the truth, his word, to draw us to Christ to make us worshippers and to sustain us in a life of worship. We need all three if we are to truly worship God: Jesus Christ, the Holy Spirit and the truth. True worship of God the Father is only possible through God the Son, by God the Spirit as we hear God's truth from his word, the Bible.

---

[3] Jn. 14:17; 15:26; 16:13.

2

The Nature of Christian Worship
'Living Sacrifices'

> [1]*Therefore, I urge you, brothers, in view of God's mercy, to offer your bodies as living sacrifices, holy and pleasing to God – this is your spiritual act of worship.* [2]*Do not conform any longer to the pattern of this world, but be transformed by the renewing of your mind. Then you will be able to test and approve what God's will is – his good, pleasing and perfect will* (Romans 12:1-2).

Jane was having a really bad day at work. It all started when one of her colleagues phoned in sick – that put the pressure on from the start. She had to take on extra jobs when she was already overloaded. Everything had to be ready for the presentation at four o'clock in the afternoon. Her stress levels were high, and they had been steadily rising throughout the day. The fact that the photocopier broke just as she needed it did not help. The last straw was the news that one of the secretaries had managed to lose a vital bit of paper with all the facts and figures she needed. She would have to go into the presentation without this information and look like a complete fool in front of everyone. Jane was furious. But just as she was about to launch a verbal attack on the secretary, she remembered what she had read in her Bible that morning – how God had forgiven her for all the dreadful things she had done. She thought to herself: 'If God is prepared to forgive me, shouldn't I forgive others?' She managed to bite her tongue and the words stayed in.

John has just arrived at college. He knows no one and is desperate to make some friends, so he goes along to as many social events as he can. He has been to all sorts of introductory meetings. Monday was the Star Trek Appreciation Society, Wednesday was the Tabasco Drinkers Society, and today is the Boat Club. He is not going to row (he is not *that* stupid), but everyone else will be there and it is a chance to meet more people. It soon becomes clear to him that the main aim of the evening is not to discuss the finer points of rowing, or even to watch Steve Redgrave videos. It is, rather, just to get drunk. John notices that all the friends he has been making over the last few days are downing pint after pint and he really wants to join in. They will not think very much of him if he switches to orange juice after a couple. There is a battle raging in his mind. Should he please his new friends and fit in with the crowd, or should he aim to please God? When he thinks of it like that, he knows what he has to do. Christ had been willing to die for him; what is a little bit of embarrassment compared to that? And so he switches to orange juice before he gets drunk.

And then there is Peter. He has been looking forward to going to church all week. He likes meeting up with everyone, but above all he loves to sing. He is in church, singing at the top of his voice: 'I love you Lord, and I lift my voice to worship you, O my soul rejoice ... I will give you all my worship, I will give you all my praise. You alone I long to worship, you alone are worthy of my praise.'

What is worship?

Which of these three people is worshipping God? Probably if we conducted a survey on the street and asked that question, the majority would be quite clear: Peter is the worshipper. The language of worship is most commonly used to speak of what takes place in church. It is not just non-Christians who speak this way. Church noticeboards invite people to 'Worship here this Sunday', with the implication that 'worship' is what happens within those four walls. As I was preparing to write this book, I came across an advert for a conference called 'Worship'. It included details of the seminars that would be offered. Every one of them was concerned with what takes place in a religious meeting: 'Liturgy and Worship', 'Celtic Worship', 'Dance Worship', 'Writing Worship Songs'. Is that all that worship is – what takes place when Christians meet together, and especially when they sing praise to God? Not according to the Bible.

I would not be surprised if some readers assumed that a book entitled *True Worship* would focus exclusively on Christian meetings. But the Bible insists that worship concerns the whole of life. Peter may be worshipping God as he sings in a church building, but so is Jane as she bites her tongue at work, and John as he switches to orange juice at the party. So please, as we think about what the Bible teaches about worship, do not stay in church in your mind. Allow your thoughts to travel to what you will be doing next Monday morning at eleven o'clock, for example, or on Saturday evening at nine o'clock. You are called to worship God wherever you are at those times as well. If we really understand what God teaches on this subject, it should have implications for everything we do, wherever we may be.

In this chapter we will look at one brief passage from Paul's letter to the Romans to see what it teaches about worship. The concept of 'worship' is very broad in the New Testament. There are four different Greek words which are sometimes translated 'worship' in our English versions of the Bible, and each of them has a slightly different meaning (we will look at them briefly in the next chapter). But Romans 12:1-2 is a good place to look for a summary of the Bible's teaching on the subject. In verse 1 Paul seems to be giving a definition of what he understands by 'worship'. He teaches that worship requires a remembrance of God's mercy, an offering of my body to God and an obedience of God's will in all parts of life.

1. Worship requires a remembrance of God's mercy

Chapter 12 verse 1 is one of the great hinges, or turning points, of Paul's magnificent letter to the Roman Christians. Chapters 1-11 focus on what God has done for sinful human beings. The theme of chapters 12-15 is what we should do in response. Paul is saying, in effect: 'God has done so much for you, now live for him.' And that is the message of verse 1. In just two words, Paul sums up all that he has said thus far in the letter. He refers to 'God's mercy'. Are you gripped by the mercy of God? If not, you will never worship him. An under-standing of God's mercy to us is the fuel that energizes and empowers our worship in all parts of life.

I have enjoyed some of the songs from the musical 'Les Miserables' for a while, but I did not know the story until someone explained it to me recently. In the novel by Victor Hugo, Jean Valjean has recently been released from jail and is looking for lodgings. That is no easy task because, in those days in France, ex-convicts had to carry special identity cards. All the innkeepers are suspicious of him and will not take him in. He spends four days wandering the streets until at last one man takes pity on him – a bishop. Valjean goes to bed, waits until the bishop is asleep and then goes around the house, looking for things he can steal. He soon finds the family silver and runs off with it.

The police soon find him with the silver and, assuming that he has stolen it, take him back to the bishop's house and knock on the door. What happens next is a shock and surprise to everyone. The bishop says: 'Ah, there you are, Valjean! How good to see you. I thought you'd be back. You must have come for the candlesticks. They're silver too. I meant you to have them as well.' Then, turning to the policemen, he says: 'You didn't think he was a thief, did you? Oh no, I gave him this silver; it's his.' The baffled gendarmes go away, leaving Valjean with his mouth wide open in disbelief. He is never the same again. The amazing generosity and grace of this bishop have such an impact on him that he is a changed man. For the rest of his life he devotes himself to helping those in need.

God's gift

Paul's letter to the Romans tells a similar story. The apostle begins by establishing the uncomfortable truth that every one of us has robbed God. God made us and has poured out his love upon us. He has given us everything that we have and enjoy, but we have robbed him of the praise, love and obedience that he alone deserves. Instead, we put other things above him and live for these things as if they were God: money, pleasure, success. We disobey God day after day after day. He could insist on the full penalty and throw us into the dungeon of hell, separated from him for ever. But instead, in his infinite love, God offers us a gift – not of silver candlesticks, but of something infinitely more precious – the gift of forgiveness and the possibility of being his friends for ever. He went to great lengths to make that possible. It cost him the death of his one and only Son, the Lord Jesus. He took the punishment that we should have faced so that, if we trust in him, we can be right with God – no matter what we have done wrong. That is the wonderful message of Romans. God offers all of us an amazing present, even though we deserve nothing but punishment from him.

Jean Valjean was never the same again after the bishop's act of kindness. Surely God's mercy to us should have an even greater impact on our lives. We should respond wholeheartedly to Paul's appeal: 'I urge you, brothers, in view of God's mercy, to offer your bodies as living sacrifices.'

We saw in the last chapter that true worship never begins with our own initiative. It is not about human beings trying to win favour from a reluctant God. It is always a response to God's initiative in sending Jesus to be our saviour. It flows out of a grateful heart as we remember what God has done for us: it is 'in view of God's mercy'.

Some Christians delight in the early years of their Christian lives to hear of Christ and his death for them on the cross. But then, as time passes, they feel it is time to graduate from that message on to something else.

They feel they need something more sophisticated. It is a dangerous mentality. Of course we need to be stretched in our thinking and seek to learn the whole counsel of God from the Scriptures. But we can never leave the basics behind. The message of God's mercy to us is not just for non-Christians and young believers. It is for all of us. We are to keep it in view throughout our lives; we will not worship God otherwise. Worship requires a remembrance of God's mercy.

2. Worship requires an offering of my body to God

In the days before Christ, God called his people to bring animal sacrifices to him in the temple. As we will see in Chapter 3, those sacrifices were always intended to be a temporary provision. They pointed beyond themselves to the one, perfect sacrifice which Christ offered when he died on the cross. The cross put an end to animal sacrifices; there was no need for them anymore. Christ's sacrifice of himself achieved all that those previous sacrifices had merely anticipated. Christ's sacrifice makes sinful human beings who trust in him totally pure in his sight and fit for a relationship with him. So we do not have to offer a sacrifice to help us stay in the right with God. Christ has done all that is necessary to achieve that. We are perfect in God's sight because of what he did for us.

But there is still a sacrifice that I am called to offer: the sacrifice of myself. In a sense, Paul is saying: 'Don't bring a sacrifice, *be one*. In response to God's mercy, offer your body to him.' That is the kind of sacrifice God wants now – not a lamb, a goat or a dove, but yourself. Such a sacrifice, says Paul, is 'holy and pleasing to him' – 'this is your spiritual act of worship'.

The mind matters

The word 'spiritual' is perhaps better translated 'reason-able' or 'rational'. The Greek word Paul uses is *logikos*, from which we get our word 'logic'. It implies that our worship is connected with our minds. That is very important for us to note. In many religions, worship and the mind are divorced. In much Eastern religion, the aim is to encounter the divine on a sub-rational level. We are encouraged to switch off our minds with the help of bodily exercises and the repetition of mantras, for exam-ple. We get in touch with the divine by submerging our consciousness. That is when worship begins.

In recent years, Eastern thinking has had a big impact on Western culture. Increasingly we are elevat-ing experience above thinking, feeling above the mind. One writer has put it like this: ours is 'a culture in search of an experience, not in search of truth'. In choosing a religion, 'The one measurement that matters is the spiritual high they give, as if worship was some-thing you snorted through your nose'.[1] That tendency has affected Christianity as well. Many people who come to church are looking for an experience. They do not want to think; they want a direct encounter with God. They want to feel his presence with them. And when they do, or at least when they think they do, they call that 'worship'. For them, worship is primarily to do with the feelings rather than with the mind. But the Bible will not allow us to divorce the two. True worship will certainly involve our emotions, but it does not begin with them. Worship is rational; it involves the mind.

---

[1] Clifford Longley, quoted in John Blanchard, *Does God Believe in Atheists?* (Darlington: Evangelical Press, 2000), 201.

One writer translates the end of verse 1: This 'is your understanding act of worship'.[2] I think that captures Paul's meaning well. Worship involves thinking because it begins with what God has done for me in Christ. It is a response to what I have understood about his mercy. If I switch my mind off, I break the connection with the truth that prompts my worship. So worship must be rational. But it can never stay just in the mind.

The body matters

Paul's use of the word 'body' tells us that he does not understand worship to be a purely intellectual, mental activity. It is not a mystical experience, inward and abstract. It is very earthy. It is about what I do with my body as I offer it, not to myself for my own gratification, but to God in his service. It is about what I say with my tongue, what I watch with my eyes, where I go with my feet, what I do with my sexual organs and my hands.

Have you begun to worship God? I am not asking if you have had a tremendous feeling in his presence. I am asking whether you have offered your body as a living sacrifice to God. Have you consciously done that? Do you recognize that we do not belong to ourselves any more? Christ gave himself up for us and in grateful, loving response we are to offer ourselves to him. Have you said in your heart: 'Lord, here I am, wholly available. I'll do anything, I'll go anywhere for you, Lord. Here's my job, my family, here are my relationships, my talents, my time at college, here's my whole body. Use it for your glory; use every part of my life?' Am I holding a part of my life back? I need to hand it over to God and say:

---

[2] David Peterson, *Engaging with God* (Leicester: IVP, 1992), 174.

'Lord, here I am. Use me for your glory as I offer the whole of myself in worship to you.'

I love the old story of the little boy who was very moved by a sermon on giving. The minister had stressed that God is the great giver and that what we give is to be in grateful response to his gift to us of his own son. When the plate was passed round for the collection, the boy looked in his pockets to see what he could contribute. He found a dirty handkerchief, a conker on a piece of string and a rusty old penknife. He did not feel that any of those items were adequate gifts in the light of all that God had given him. He hesitated for a moment while he held the plate in his hands, then he put it on the floor and stepped into it. That is worship: the offering of our whole selves, our bodies, to God.

3. Worship involves an obedience to God's will in all parts of life

Having urged us to offer our bodies to God, Paul spells out what that will mean in practice. He continues: 'Do not conform any longer to the pattern of this world, but be transformed by the renewing of your mind.' If we are to worship God properly, we must be prepared to be non-conformists, to stand out and be different. J.B. Phillips translated verse 2: 'Don't let the world around you squeeze you into its own mould, but let God remould you from within.' That is not easy. Anyone can sing with great gusto on a Sunday: 'All that I am, I lay before you'; 'I will offer up my life in spirit and truth, pouring out the oil of love as my worship to you.' But worship is not so easy on a Monday morning or a Saturday evening, when you are surrounded by colleagues or friends who have no desire to live God's way.

You cannot judge a church's worship by what happens in the hour or so when they meet on a Sunday. The real test is how its members behave during the rest of the week. Are they conformists who fit into the world's mould? Or are they true worshippers who obey God? What about you? How do you live?

'The first two verses of Romans 12 place the concluding chapters of the letter under the umbrella of worship.'[3] Paul gives us a worship checklist. There are no questions about our instruments or amplification. He probes instead into our daily lives. In Romans 12 and 13 Paul tells us what a life of worship will mean in a series of different relationships. How is your worship when judged against his standards?

A worship checklist

1) Your relationship with yourself (Rom. 12:3-8)

'Do not think of yourself more highly than you ought, but rather think of yourself with sober judgment.' (v. 3)

Are you secretly rather full of yourself? 'Look how well I'm doing at work or at college. And I play an important role in the church. My commitment sets the standard for everyone else; that Holiday Club could never have happened without me.' But, while we pat ourselves on the back, we should pause and think. Who gave us the qualities and abilities we have? God did. Should he not be the one getting all the praise?

2) Your relationship with other Christians (Rom. 12:9-16)

'Be devoted to one another in brotherly love.' (v. 10)

Is meeting with your brothers and sisters a top priority, or do you only go to church when there is

---

[3] Peterson, *Engaging*, 178.

nothing else on? And how do you treat others when you do meet? Are you only interested in those you instantly warm to, or do you make an effort to get to know others as well? And when you become aware of needs, do you seek to meet them? When someone is lonely, do you invite them round? When another needs to talk, do you listen? Love must involve more than smiling at someone on a Sunday. We each need to ask ourselves the question: am I prepared to put myself out for others?

3) Your relationship with your enemies (Rom. 12:17-21)

'Do not repay anyone evil for evil' (v. 17).

Perhaps your neighbour did keep you up until two o'clock last night with that wretched music. But does that really give you an excuse to play the radio at full volume at seven o'clock in the morning, or to block their drive with your car? Perhaps someone has wronged you in the past. Will you go on nursing that grievance or will you ask for God's help to forgive?

4) Your relationship to authorities (Rom. 13:1-7)

'Everyone must submit himself to the governing authorities, for there is no authority except that which God has established.' (v. 1)

Paul here is speaking first and foremost of the state. We are all to obey the law of the land, even when it does not suit us. We should pay our taxes scrupulously and in full. But there are wider applications, too. You may think it is ridiculous that your boss insists you are always at your desk by nine o'clock – but if he says it, you should do it. You may find it inconvenient that the college requires you to pay bills by a certain date, but once again, we should obey.

5) Your relationship to God's standards (Rom. 13:8-14)

'Let us behave decently, as in the daytime, not in orgies and drunkenness, not in sexual immorality

and debauchery, not in dissension and jealousy.'
(v. 13)

People will say: 'It's fine to get drunk – everyone
does it. You've got to let your hair down every now
and then. And for goodness sake don't confine sex to
marriage! That's so old-fashioned. Don't be such a
prude. Experiment, enjoy yourself.' Am I going to
conform to the way of the world and go along with
my sinful desires? Or will I worship God? That is the
issue.

Offering my body to God is not just something I do
as I sing on a Sunday and can then forget about for the
rest of the week. It must be worked out in practice,
day by day, hour by hour. A friend of mine has put it
like this: 'To say, "I'm going to church to worship", is
about as silly as saying, "I'm off to bed to breathe for
a while".' Worship should define the whole of my life.

We all need to remember God's mercy towards us.
And then, in grateful response, we should offer our
bodies to God, making sure that that offering is
worked out in practice in all parts of life. Ruth
Graham, Billy's wife, placed a card above the kitchen
sink at home. It said: 'Divine worship offered here,
three times daily.' Perhaps you could echo those
words as you go to the office tomorrow morning, or
start the ironing, or go to that party: 'Divine worship
offered here'. What a difference it would make to all
of our lives if we really understood that.

3

The End of Religion
'He sat down'

'Where do you worship?' The correct answer to this question is not 'Christ Church', or 'St Saviour's', but 'everywhere'. You could be accused of being pedantic if you gave that reply, but you would be right. We have seen that worship is not limited to what happens in church on a Sunday. It involves responding to God's mercy to us in Christ by offering ourselves fully to him in obedient service in all parts of life, wherever we are, every day of the week. So why do Christians meet together? We will address that question in this chapter and in Chapter 4. This chapter will give a negative answer: we do not meet specifically to worship God. Chapter 4 will be more positive: we meet to encourage one another.

You might think it strange that I should devote an entire chapter to making a negative point, but I think it will be time well spent. There is a great deal of unbiblical thinking among Christians in this area that needs to be challenged by God's word. Many people believe that the reason we gather as believers is to worship God. Our

language reflects our understanding. We speak of
'Morning Worship' or an 'Evening Service'. But the Bible
never defines Christian meetings in those terms.

Worship words

I mentioned in the last chapter that there are four main
Greek words in the New Testament that are often translated 'worship' in our English versions. It is striking that
these words are hardly ever used to describe what happens in Christian meetings, and they are never used to
speak of the purpose of those meetings. We will look at
each word briefly.

Prostration/rendering homage (**proskuneo**)

Proskuneo is the Greek word most frequently translated
'worship' in our Bibles. It literally means 'to come
towards to kiss'. The word was used to describe the
practice of expressing homage by falling down before a
superior and kissing his feet, the hem of his robe, or the
ground. It was also used to describe the inner attitude of
homage and respect that the action expressed. The Magi
travelled from the east so that they might 'worship' the
newborn king of the Jews.[1] And, after encountering the
risen Jesus, the disciples 'clasped his feet and worshipped him'.[2] Jesus uses the same word when he speaks
of the new kind of worship that he will make possible:
'the true worshippers will worship the Father in spirit
and truth'.[3] We learn from the book of Revelation that
such worship is already being offered perfectly in

[1] Mt. 2:2.
[2] Mt. 28:9.
[3] Jn. 4:23.

heaven.[4] The book of Revelation is an appeal to us on earth to not worship the beast, but rather to worship God alone.[5] That means submitting to him and giving him our undivided allegiance.

Proskuneo is only used on one occasion in connection with a church meeting . And in that case it describes, not what Christians do, but rather the conversion of a non-Christian. In 1 Corinthians 14:25 Paul says that the unbeliever who is convicted by a prophetic word will 'fall down and worship God, exclaiming, "God is really among you!"'

Service (leitourgeo)

The Greek words related to *leitourgeo* speak of duties performed before God. Jewish priests and angels are both described as 'serving' or 'worshipping' God as they carry out their functions.[6] But the New Testament does not use these words in an exclusively 'religious' sense. Even secular rulers 'serve' God as they fulfil their responsibility to govern.[7] Paul sees the whole of his evangelistic work to the Gentiles as service of Christ,[8] and he uses words from the same word group to speak of the faith of the Philippians.[9] 'Service' is certainly not restricted to church. Indeed, the New Testament only uses this word on one occasion to speak of what happens in a church meeting, where it probably refers to prayer.[10]

---

[4] Rev. 4:10; 7:11; etc.
[5] Rev. 14:6-7; 19:10; 22:8-9.
[6] E.g., Heb. 1:6; 8:2.
[7] Rom. 13:6.
[8] Rom. 15:16.
[9] Phil. 2:17.
[10] Acts 13:2.

Respect/reverence (**sebomai**)

This word is used to describe the respect or reverence that human beings show to God. The most common usage is in connection with Gentile 'God-fearers' who participated in synagogue life.[11] The New Testament also uses the word to describe the religious activities of non-Christians,[12] but only once does it refer to what Christians do when they meet together – and then it is used by non-Christians.[13]

Obediencel adoration (**latreuo**)

Latreuo is used to speak of the adoration offered to God in heaven[14] and the temple worship of the Jews.[15] But, as with the other worship words, it is not limited to a narrow religious reference. Paul described his missionary work as worship[16] and Jesus predicted that some would even regard the persecution of Christians in the same way.[17] More broadly, the word is used to describe Christians serving God with their whole lives.[18] The offering of our bodies to God is our 'spiritual act of worship'.[19]

We do not go to church to worship

This quick look at the worship language of the New Testament makes it clear that worship involves the

[11] E.g., Acts 13:43; 16:14.
[12] Acts 17:23; 19:27.
[13] Acts 18:13.
[14] Rev. 7:15; 22:3.
[15] E.g., Heb. 8:5; 13:10.
[16] Acts 24:14; 27:23.
[17] Jn. 16:2.
[18] 2 Tim. 1:3; Heb. 9:14.
[19] Rom. 12:1.

whole of our lives. Whereas we often restrict the terminology to speak of what we do when we meet together as Christians, the Bible never does.

Howard Marshall wrote an important article entitled: 'How Far Did the Early Christians Worship God?' He states:

> It is true that Christian meetings can be described from the outside as occasions for worshipping God and also that elements of service to God took place in them, but the remarkable fact is that Christian meetings are not said to take place specifically to worship God and the language of worship is not used as a means of referring to them or describing them. To sum up what goes on in a Christian meeting as being specifically for the purpose of 'worship' is without New Testament precedent. 'Worship' is not an umbrella-term for what goes on when Christians gather together.[20]

We often assume that the main reason we meet as Christians is to offer worship to God, but the New Testament does not speak in those terms. It teaches that the prime direction of our meetings is not from us to God, but rather from him to us. How have we got it so wrong? The answer is that we are still stuck in the Old Testament in our thinking. We have failed to grasp the significance of the coming of Jesus. He put an end to religion and it is about time we realized it.

Old covenant religion

In the old covenant days, before Christ came, much worship of God was centred on the temple in Jerusalem. He

---

[20] 'How Far Did the Early Christians Worship God?', *Churchman 99* (1985), 220.

focused his presence right at the heart of that temple in the Most Holy Place. If the Israelites wanted to draw near to him, they had to approach him there. But they could not simply stroll into his presence. They could only approach him through mediators, known as priests.

I was fourteen and at the height of my addiction to cricket when I received a wonderful invitation. I was invited to the Oval cricket ground in London to watch a match between England and India. My host also told me that, if I went to the door of the pavilion at teatime, I would be allowed in and would be introduced to some England players. I was very excited. The pavilion was hallowed ground as far as I was concerned – few were admitted. And meeting some of the game's greatest players was a thrilling prospect for a star-struck teenager.

But how would I ever get into that pavilion? Security guards were posted at the door to ensure that only members were admitted. I should not have worried. I went to the door at the appointed hour and was met there by my host and a friend of his called Godfrey Evans. I am afraid that the significance of that name might be lost on some readers. If you had the misfortune to be brought up in a country that does not play cricket, you can be forgiven. Otherwise you should know that Godfrey Evans was one of the greatest players England has ever known. The man guarding the door recognized him right away. He would normally have taken delight in shooing me away but, because I was with Godfrey, I was ushered straight in. He was my mediator – I could not have entered without him.

That was the role the priests played in the old covenant. God was so holy, and the people were so sinful that they could not simply walk into his presence. They would be barred from entry every time. They could only approach him through mediators – priests. And those priests first had to offer sacrifices. The people deserved the punishment of death for their disobedience of God. But, in his mercy, God allowed animals to be killed instead, as substitutes. The sacrifices thus achieved atonement, at-one-ment, between the holy God and sinful people. But, as we will see, this atonement was not perfect: the Israelites' access to God was very limited. They needed a better mediator.

The main direction of the activity in the temple was from human beings to God, as they offered sacrifices to him through priests. But that should not be the model for Christian meetings any more. Jesus brought the whole temple system to an end. He fulfilled it. The temple and its sacrifices were only designed by God to be a temporary provision. They pointed beyond themselves to what Christ came to achieve. The book of Hebrews stresses this particularly.

The book of Hebrews

Hebrews was written to Jewish Christians who were facing persecution. As a result of this persecution, they were tempted to drift from Christ and return to their former religion. The writer pleads with them not to do so. He reminds them that what they have in Christ is far better than what they had before. The temple and its rituals were never designed to be permanent. It was just a 'copy' of the real thing, a 'shadow' compared with the substance which came with Christ.[21]

The present I always dreaded as a child was an Airfix model aeroplane kit. I am completely ham-fisted and

---

[21] Heb. 8:5; 9:24; 10:1.

found it impossible to connect the pieces together to produce the impressive-looking aeroplane shown on the packet. But, for reasons that I still struggle to understand, some of my friends loved those kits. They enjoyed making them and then playing with the finished product. Their planes looked quite impressive, but none of my friends were foolish enough to think that they could really fly. They were just models.

The writer to the Hebrews wants his readers to understand that the old covenant system of religion was also a model. It could not do the job of establishing a perfect relationship with God. Only the work of Christ made that relationship possible. He is a perfect priest who offered a perfect sacrifice and achieved perfect access to God.

A perfect priest

Christ suffered from none of the limitations of the priests of the old covenant. They were always needing to be replaced because of death. But Jesus lives for ever:

> *There have been many of those priests, since death prevented them from continuing in office; but because Jesus lives for ever, he has a permanent priesthood. Therefore, he is able to save completely those who come to God through him, because he always lives to intercede for them.* (Heb. 7:23-25)

The priests of the old covenant were hampered, not just by their mortality, but also by their own sinfulness. They were part of the problem, so they could never achieve a solution and bring people to God. But Jesus was different. He is:

Holy, blameless, pure, set apart from sinners, exalted above the heavens. Unlike the other high priests, he does not need to offer sacrifices day after day, first for his own sins, and then for the sins of the people. ... For the law appoints as high priests men who are weak; but the oath, which came after the law, appointed the Son, who has been made perfect for ever. (Heb. 7:26-28)

And whereas the other priests ministered in the temple on earth, Christ performed his ministry in heaven itself. The Jewish high priest entered the Most Holy Place in the temple in Jerusalem. But Jesus went to heaven:

We do have such a high priest, who sat down at the right hand of the throne of the Majesty in heaven, and who serves in the sanctuary, the true tabernacle set up by the Lord, not by man. (Heb. 8:1-2)

The perfect sacrifice

Jesus also offered a perfect sacrifice. The priests in the temple offered animal sacrifices. The fact that they had to be repeated over and over again testified to the fact that they were not effective in dealing with the problem of human sin:

The law is only a shadow of the good things that are coming – not the realities themselves. For this reason it can never, by the same sacrifices repeated endlessly year after year, make perfect those who draw near to worship. If it could, would they not have stopped being offered? For the worshippers would have been cleansed once for all, and would no longer have felt guilty for their sins. But those sacrifices are an annual reminder of sins, because it is impossible for the blood of bulls and goats to take away sins. (Heb.10:1-4)

The death of an animal is not an adequate substitute for a human being.

There used to be a programme on British television called 'The Krypton Factor'. Contestants were given a series of difficult tasks to complete, including a puzzle to solve. As soon as they were finished, they sat down. The first to do so won. As long as they remained standing, they made public that they had not finished the job.

The writer to the Hebrews points out that the task of dealing with sin was not completed by the old covenant priests. They remained standing. But Jesus achieved what they could never do:

> *Day after day every priest stands and performs his religious duties; again and again he offers the same sacrifices, which can never take away sins. But when this priest [Jesus] had offered for all time one sacrifice for sins, he sat down at the right hand of God.* (Heb. 10:11-12)

Jesus succeeded where the other priests had failed because he offered a different kind of sacrifice: 'He sacrificed for their sins once for all when he offered himself' (Heb. 7:27). He is both the priest and the sacrifice. No animal can ever be an adequate substitute for a human being. But Jesus is the perfect substitute. He perfectly represented sinful humanity and stood in for us when he died on the cross. And, because he himself was without sin, he was able to pay the price for ours. His was a perfect sacrifice that never needs to be repeated. It has been offered 'once for all' (Heb. 9:26) and 'for all time' (Heb. 10:12).

Perfect access

The Israelites did enjoy a relationship with God, but it was a distant one. The temple proclaimed the nearness of God, but it also reminded them of how remote he still was. Under the old covenant, access into God's presence was very limited:

> ...*only the high priest entered the inner room, and that only once a year ... The Holy Spirit was showing by this that the way into the Most Holy Place had not yet been disclosed.* (Heb. 9:7-8)

The temple was a massive 'No Entry!' sign.

But everything is different now. If worship in the old covenant days took place in 'an earthly sanctuary' (Heb. 9:1), the focus in the new covenant is heaven itself. 'Christ did not enter a man-made sanctuary that was only a copy of the true one; he entered heaven itself, now to appear for us in God's presence' (Heb. 9:24). Because, as the perfect priest, he took the blood of his perfect sacrifice for us into the very presence of his Father in heaven, the 'No Entry!' sign has been thrown away. Christ has opened up perfect access to God. That fact was vividly proclaimed at the moment of Jesus' death when the curtain in the temple, which separated the Most Holy Place from the rest of the building, was torn in two.[22]

The door back to God is now wide open. We do not have to go to some holy place and find a priest who will offer up a sacrifice for us. Christ has already done everything necessary to bring us to God. There is nothing more for us to do except trust in what Jesus has done for us. The writer to the Hebrews concludes his argument with an appeal:

> *Therefore, brothers, since we have confidence to enter the Most Holy Place by the blood of Jesus, by a new and living way*

---

[22] Mk. 15:38.

opened for us through the curtain, that is, his body, and since
we have a great priest over the house of God, let us draw near
to God with a sincere heart in full assurance of faith, having
our hearts sprinkled to cleanse us from a guilty conscience.
(Heb. 10:19-22)

The implications for worship are massive. Under the old
covenant, worship, or 'service', did take place when
God's people gathered on earth.[23] Worship offered to
God was the main focus of the activity in the earthly
sanctuary. But all that was fulfilled by the worship, or
service, of the Lord Jesus, when he offered himself as a
perfect sacrifice to his Father. In the new covenant the
emphasis is not on our worship on earth, but on Christ's
in heaven. Because of his act of worship, his self-offering, there is no longer any need for holy places, mediating priests, or atoning sacrifices. In that sense, at least, he
put an end to religion and we must not try to revive it.

No more holy places

The Hebrew Christians were tempted to return to religion, and we often are as well. We speak of our buildings as if they were holy places. We set a part of them
aside as 'the sanctuary'. But since Christ's death there
have been no holy places. If we want to meet with God
we do not need to go to any temple on earth. Instead, we
are simply to trust in Christ, who offers us direct access
to his Father in heaven.

There are more Christians in China than in any other
country. Most of them are members of illegal house
churches. They have no church buildings and meet in

---

[23] Heb. 9:1.

small groups in members' homes. Are they missing out on something important? Of course not. Often our buildings have been a hindrance rather than a help. They can require large sums of money for maintenance that might be better used to employ workers, and they can be inconveniently located for us to reach people. Often, of course, our buildings help us in our work. If so, we should thank God for them; but let us not invest them with any religious significance. One church leader likes to remind his congregation that their building is 'just a rain shelter'. God does not live there, and we should avoid any decoration or terminology which implies that he does. Our focus should be on the perfect sanctuary in heaven where Christ is, rather than on any building on earth.

No more priests

Because Christ is the perfect priest, we do not need anyone else to help bridge the gap between us and God. The New Testament encourages us to go straight to God through Christ. It never points us to any other priest. It does speak of all believers as priests in the sense that we are called to represent God to an unbelieving world: we are 'a royal priesthood'.[24] But it never speaks of a special caste of Christians whose function it is to stand between God and other believers. And yet that is how the priest is viewed in traditional Catholic thinking. Pope Pius XII once wrote:

> *The sacrament of order sets priests in a class apart from all other Christians ... They are made divine instruments to*

---

[24] 1 Pet. 2:9.

communicate the heavenly and supernatural life in the mystical body of Jesus Christ. It is to priests, then, that all must have recourse who want to live in Christ.[25]

That is a direct contradiction of the words of the apostle Paul: 'There is one mediator between God and men: the man Christ Jesus.'[26]

I preached an early version of this chapter at church in Oxford. One man was clearly agitated and walked out as I stated that there is no longer a need for any group to be set apart as priests in the church. He waited for me afterwards and told me that he was so angry that he could hardly speak. It turned out that he was training to be ordained in the Church of England. He understood his future ministry as a 'priesthood' and was deeply upset by what I had said: 'How dare you presume to sweep away a whole order of ministry in just a few words.' But it was not my words that swept it away; Christ's death did. There is no longer any need for a special order of mediating priests.

'Priest' is not the Bible's word for Christian leaders. It speaks of 'elders', 'overseers' or 'pastor-teachers'.[27] It is unfortunate that the Anglican reformers continued to use 'priest' as a title for gospel ministers. They justified this by pointing out that it was simply a conflation of 'presbyter', the Greek word for 'elder'. They may have been right etymologically, but it was not a wise decision. The continued use of 'priest' as a description of Christian leaders has led to confusion and error. We need no priest but Christ to bring us to God and then to keep us in right relationship with him.

---

[25] H.M. Carson, *Dawn or Twilight* (Leicester: IVP, 1976), 94.

[26] 1 Tim. 2:5.

[27] E.g., Eph. 4:11; Tit. 1:6-7.

No more atoning sacrifices

Christ's perfect sacrifice means that no other sacrifice is necessary to make us right with God. When we meet together as believers, we do not need to offer anything to God to improve our relationship with him. The New Testament does refer to sacrifices that we offer as Christians. They include giving praise, and the offering of our lives to God.[28] But none of those sacrifices secure a relationship with God; they do not achieve atonement. They are simply responses to the one perfect sacrifice Christ offered for us.

Christ's sacrifice has made it possible for us to be completely acceptable to God. There is nothing more for us to do. And yet Roman Catholic theologians speak of the Lord's Supper, 'the mass', as in some sense a re-offering of the sacrifice of Christ. So, for many people, the focal point of a church meeting is the offering of a sacrifice by a priest at the altar in the mass. That is a return to old covenant days. The prime direction of the proceedings is from us to God, as it was then. But that is not the prime direction envisaged by the New Testament in the celebration of the Lord's Supper. We will return to this theme in Chapter 6.

We should not think that it is only those within the Catholic tradition who act as if they are still in the old covenant. It is also a danger within some understandings of worship in the evangelical world. I read these words of a Christian band recently: 'Songs that lift up the name of Jesus, combined with music that moves the body, provide an avenue for the listener to enter into the presence of God.' That reflects a common understanding. Music, it is believed, can draw us close to God.

[28] Rom. 12:1; Phil. 2:17; 4:8; Heb. 13;15-16; 1 Pet. 2:5.

Some people feel that they do not really meet with God if there is not an extended time of singing in every meeting. The 'worship leader' is expected to exercise an almost priestly function and take us into God's presence. I will say more on the subject of music in Chapter 5. We will see there that the Bible never teaches that it is the role of music to lead us closer to God.

No worship we offer, whether in praise or in the sacrament, can bring us to God. We depend entirely on the worship Jesus offered when he died on the cross, offering his life as a sacrifice. In Christ we are already in God's presence.[29] There is nothing for us to do except draw near with faith. We do not have to offer the mass or sing for half an hour to draw close to God. We are already close to him if we have trusted in Christ – in fact, we could not be closer to him.

So let us not go back to the ways of the old covenant. Christ has brought an end to religion. If we grasp that great truth we will see why the New Testament does not teach that we meet together to worship God.

---

[29] Heb. 12:22.

4

The Purpose of Christian Meetings
'Encourage one another'

Why do Christians meet together? In the last chapter we looked at the negative answer: we do not meet in order to worship God. Although our actions in church meetings can be described as worship because we should be worshipping at all times, the New Testament does not speak of believers gathering for the express purpose of worship. Now it is time to look at the positive answer the Bible gives to our question. It teaches that Christians are to meet primarily for the purpose of encouragement.

Hebrews: Encouragement

Under the old covenant, God's people had gathered together to offer sacrifices to him through priests in the temple. The writer to the Hebrews stresses that there is no need for such 'worship' any more. And yet he still urges us to meet with one another:

> ... *let us consider how we may spur one another on towards love and good deeds. Let us not give up meeting together, as*

*some are in the habit of doing, but let us encourage one
another – and all the more as you see the Day approaching.*
(Heb. 10:24-25)

Notice how the writer's vision is dominated by what he
calls 'the Day'. That is the day to which all history is heading, the moment when Christ returns. Until then it will
always be difficult to follow Christ. We have received so
much from him, including the right of access into God's
presence. We can be sure that he is with us in our trials.
He understands what we are going through and he for-
gives us when we fall.[1] But we only know those blessings
through faith. We do not see God face to face; we must
wait until Christ's return for that. Until then our salvation
is incomplete – at least in our experience.

It is hard being a Christian while we wait for 'the
Day'. That is why we need to meet together: to 'spur one
another on' and to 'encourage one another'. There is a
great danger that I will give up in the Christian life
before I reach the finishing line. That is why I need you
– you are God's provision for me to keep me going. I
need you, and you need me.

I like the emphasis in Hebrews. The writer could have
said: 'Make sure you keep meeting other believers, otherwise you could easily fall away.' That would have
been true. But instead he chooses to put the emphasis in
the other direction: 'Keep meeting up with other
Christians, not so much for your sake as for theirs – they
need your encouragement.' The same point is made earlier in the letter:

*See to it, brothers, that none of you has a sinful, unbelieving
heart that turns away from the living God. But encourage*

---

[1] Heb. 4:18; 9:14.

one another daily, as long as it is called Today, so that none of you may be hardened by sin's deceitfulness (Heb. 3:12-13).

Paul: Edification

Paul has a similar understanding to that of the writer to the Hebrews, but he tends to refer to 'edification' rather than encouragement. The verb he uses, *oikodomein*, was a standard word for building houses or other structures. In Paul's letters it describes the building up of churches. We are not simply a collection of individuals. Churches are corporate entities. The New Testament images for churches make that point. We are a family, God's temple, and the body of Christ.[2] We are bound together and are expected to grow together towards Christian maturity. Our meetings should serve that end. Paul writes to the Thessalonians: 'Encourage one another and build each other up.'[3]

Edification was so central to Paul's understanding of the purpose of Christian meetings that it provided the test as to whether something should be included in them or not. The question he wants us to ask about every aspect of our meetings is: 'Is it edifying?' 'Does it build people up as believers?' That principle underlies the whole of his argument in 1 Corinthians 14. He makes it clear that he approves of speaking in tongues, but uninterpreted tongues should have no place in church gatherings. The practice may help an individual praise God, but no one else receives any benefit: 'You may be giving thanks well enough, but the other man is not edified' (v. 17). He urges the Corinthians to 'try to excel in gifts that build up the church' (v. 12).

---

[2] 1 Pet. 1:22; 2:4-5; 1 Cor. 12;12-13.
[3] 1 Thess. 5:11.

A. From God to us

The New Testament's emphasis is, therefore, that Christians are to meet together to encourage one another and to build each other up. While in our meetings we are directing ourselves primarily towards one another rather than towards God, God's involvement is essential. It is he who provides the encouragement and edification that we so desperately need. First and foremost, it is God who serves us when we meet rather than we who serve him. He ministers to us through his word, the sacraments and the spiritual gifts he gives to every member.

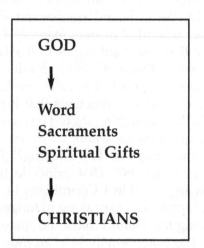

GOD

↓

Word
Sacraments
Spiritual Gifts

↓

CHRISTIANS

1. God's word

It is above all by his word that God encourages us and builds us up as believers. The ministry of God's word must be at the heart of our meetings. Without that word, we cannot claim to be Christian churches.

God's word creates the church

There was much debate at the time of the Reformation in the sixteenth century concerning what constituted a true church. Roman Catholic theologians insisted that the new Protestant churches were not true churches because they had broken fellowship with Rome and were therefore not within the apostolic succession. This charge forced the Reformers to look to their Bibles to find the marks of a true church (*notae ecclesiae*). They came to the conclusion that there was really only one vital ingredient, without which a true church could not exist: the presence of Christ. This conviction then led them to ask how Christ was present as a group met. Of course, in one sense he is always present everywhere. He is especially present, however, as his word is proclaimed. Without the preaching of the biblical gospel there can be no true church. The presence of the gospel, the word of God, ensures the presence of Christ.

It is through God's word that that we come to know Christ in the first place. Paul wrote to the Ephesians: '... you ... were included in Christ when you heard the word of truth, the gospel of your salvation' (Eph. 1:13). It is possible to have a Christian church without a church building, ordained ministers and music. It is even possible to have a church without sacraments. But there can be no true church without the gospel. Jesus himself said: 'My sheep listen to my voice' (Jn. 10:27). Martin Luther wrote, no doubt with that verse in mind: 'Thank God, even a seven-year-old child knows what the church is, namely, holy believers and sheep who hear the voice of the shepherd.'[4] John Calvin teaches much the same: 'The

---

[4] Quoted in Paul Avis, *The Church and the Theology of the Reformers* (London: Marshall, Morgan and Scott, 1981), 20.

church is seen where Christ appears and where his word is heard.'[5]

God's word builds the church

If God's word is vital for the creation of a church, it is also vital for its edification. John Stott expresses that truth powerfully:

> God's new creation (the Church) is as dependent upon his Word as his old creation (the universe). Not only has he brought it into being by his Word, but he maintains and sustains it, directs and sanctifies it, reforms and renews it through the same Word. The Word of God is the sceptre by which Christ rules the Church and the food with which he nourishes it.[6]

Peter, speaking of God's word, urges Christians: 'Like newborn babies, crave pure spiritual milk, so that by it you may grow up in your salvation' (1 Pet. 2:2). Ministry of the word had a crucial place in the meetings of the early Christians. Luke tells us that after the day of Pentecost believers 'devoted themselves to the apostles' teaching' (Acts 2:42). The sharing of God's word was the responsibility of all church members. Paul writes to the Colossians: 'Let the word of Christ dwell in you richly as you teach and admonish one another' (Col. 3:16). It is as all 'speak the truth in love' that they 'grow up into him who is the Head, that is, Christ (Eph. 4:15). We should all look for opportunities to encourage one another in the faith by reminding each other of God's truth. From the

---

[5] Avis, *The Church*, 33.
[6] John Stott, *I Believe in Preaching* (London: Hodder & Stoughton, 1982), 109.

very beginning, however, some Christians were recognized as having special gifts in proclaiming God's word and were given particular responsibility for that task. Both teachers and prophets were active in the first century.

Prophets and teachers

The nature of Christian prophecy is a hotly debated subject, and there is little space here to examine all the arguments. In 1 Corinthians 14 Paul encourages Christians to seek the gift of prophecy rather than the gift of tongues because it is so useful in the edification of the church.[7] 'Everyone who prophesies speaks to men for their strengthening, encouragement and comfort' (v. 3). Prophecy in this context appears to have the same effect as teaching. Paul was writing at a time when much of the New Testament had not yet been written. The early church therefore depended to a significant extent on the ministry of prophets through whom God revealed his truth. Paul tells us elsewhere that these prophets, along with the apostles, formed the foundation of the church. He speaks of God's household, 'built on the foundation of the apostles and prophets, with Christ Jesus himself as the chief cornerstone' (Eph. 2:20). The prophets to whom he refers cannot be Old Testament prophets as they have only just received God's revelation:

> ... *the mystery of Christ ... was not made known to men in other generations as it has now been revealed by the Spirit to God's holy apostles and prophets.*[8]

---

[7] 1 Cor. 14:1-5.
[8] (Eph. 3: 4-5)

In the earliest days of the church the apostolic gospel, therefore, came through the ministry of prophets, who received direct revelation from God, as well as through teachers, who explained the Old Testament Scriptures or the teaching of the apostles. Now that the foundation has been laid and the New Testament has been completed, there is no need for more prophets of this kind. That need not mean that there is no continuing gift of prophecy today, but it no longer has the same significance as it had in the first century. We have a sufficient revelation from God in the completed Scriptures.

When Paul faced imminent death he wrote to his young disciple, Timothy, with instructions about how he was to minister to God's people. The instructions are significant as they give us an insight into Paul's understanding of pastoral ministry in the post-apostolic days. There is no indication that Timothy and his successors (Christian pastors through the ages) are to look for new revelation from God. They are, rather, to protect the revelation they have already received from the apostles, which is now preserved in the New Testament, and proclaim it to others:

> *What you heard from me, keep as the pattern of sound teaching … Guard the good deposit that was entrusted to you.* (2 Tim.1:13-14)

> *… the things you have heard me say in the presence of many witnesses entrust to reliable men who will also be qualified to teach others.* (2 Tim. 2:2)

> *Preach the word; be prepared in season and out of season; correct, rebuke and encourage – with great patience and careful instruction.* (2 Tim. 4:2)

Churches today desperately need many more pastors who will obey the instructions Paul gave to Timothy. Christians in many parts of the world have remained stunted in their growth because they have nobody to teach them God's word. We should pray urgently for God to raise up more teachers. Perhaps you could be an answer to your own prayer. And if you have responsibility for organizing any Christian meeting, make sure that ample time is given to hearing God speak through his word. That is his chief way of building us up. I have been to churches and Christian Unions where it seems that the word of God is only given whatever time happens to be left over after the singing, Lord's Supper, notices and much else besides. We must heed the warning: 'A deaf church is a dead church: that is an unalterable principle.'[9]

2. Sacraments

The Lord Jesus instituted two sacraments: baptism and the Lord's Supper. They are two other means by which God ministers to us when we meet and encourage us in our faith. Once more, the prime direction is not from us to God, but rather from him to us. Baptism is not, first and foremost, the believer waving at God and saying: 'Look, I'm a Christian now!' Baptism speaks of God's grace, not our faith. It is a declaration of what God has done for his people: cleansing us from our sin and giving us new life. Likewise, the Lord's Supper is not something we offer to God. It is a proclamation of the gospel from him to us. It signifies both the offer and the gift of salvation in Christ.

---

[9] Stott, *I Believe*, 113.

That is all I propose to say about the sacraments here. That is partly because we will return to the theme of the Lord's Supper in more detail in Chapter 6. It is also because I have already said much of what I would want to say about the sacraments in the discussion of God's word above. The sacraments are best seen not as a separate means by which God encourages us as Christians but as one form of the ministry of his word.

John Stott makes the point well:

> ... Augustine's designation of the sacraments as 'visible words' (*verba visibilia*) supplies an essential clue to their function and value. They too speak. Both Word and sacrament bear witness to Christ. Both promise salvation in Christ. Both quicken our faith in Christ. Both enable us to feed on Christ in our hearts. The major difference between them is that the message of the one is directed to the eye, and of the other to the ear. So the sacraments need the Word to interpret them. The ministry of Word and sacrament is a single ministry, the Word proclaiming, and the sacrament dramatizing, God's promises. Yet the Word is primary, since without it the sign becomes dark in meaning, if not actually dumb.[10]

3. Spiritual gifts

I once read these words in a newspaper interview with a distinguished lawyer:

> When I go to church I want to pray and worship God and I'm doing it myself. I'm not very interested in who

---

[10] Stott, *I Believe*, 114.

else is there, and I'm afraid that I can't abide it
when someone wants to shake my hand in the middle of
it all.[11]

He has completely misunderstood the purpose of
Christian meetings. We do not go to church as individuals to worship God; we go as a body to encourage one
another. We all have a vital part to play.

Mutual ministry

There is a danger that my earlier comments about the
significance of Bible teachers could have given the
impression that they are the only significant people in
God's work of building up churches. That is certainly
not what the New Testament says. Teachers play a crucial role, but not at the expense of the contributions of
others. In fact, the the ministry of teachers is designed by
God to be the catalyst that enables others to play their
part. That is clear from what Paul says in Ephesians
4:11-13:

> It was he [the ascended Christ] who gave some to be apostles,
> some to be prophets, some to be evangelists, and some to be
> pastors and teachers, to prepare God's people for works of
> service, so that the body of Christ may be built up until we
> all reach unity in the faith and in the knowledge of the Son of
> God and become mature, attaining to the whole measure of
> the fullness of Christ.

Follow the logic as we work backwards through those
verses. What is Paul's goal for churches? That we are
built up and become mature (vv. 12b, 13). And how is

---

[11] 'The Door', March 1991.

that to happen? As God's people do their 'works of service' or, more literally, their 'ministry' (v. 12a). It is not just a special group of people in a church who are the ministers. All God's people have that responsibility. A church is built up as all its members minister to one another.

But how is it that church members will be mobilized to do that work? How will they be prepared for their works of service? They will be prepared for their works of service through the work of those gifted in word ministry: apostles and prophets (who were active in the foundation period of the church)[12] as well as evangelists and pastor-teachers.[13] It is as God's word is taught to a congregation that its members are equipped to serve each other. I have seen it often. Sleepy churches come alive when God's word begins to be taught. As individuals grow in their knowledge and love of Christ, they have a new concern for others in the fellowship. And the more they grow, the better able they are to help others in their Christian lives. The whole church begins to grow in maturity as more and more people are looking out for one another and meeting each other's needs.

That is how the Bible expects churches to be built up. There is certainly a need for suitably gifted leaders to be set apart for pastoral ministry, but the spiritual growth of churches does not depend on them alone. Again and again the New Testament exhorts all church members to be involved in ministry to one another:

'Love one another.' (Rom. 13:8)

'Encourage one another.' (1 Thess. 5:11)

'Spur one another on towards love and good deeds.' (Heb. 10:24)

'Offer hospitality to one another.' (1 Pet. 4:9)

---

[12] See Eph. 2:20 and 3:4-5.

[13] Most scholars believe Paul was referring to one group of people when he spoke of 'pastors and teachers'.

'Teach and admonish one another.' (Col. 3:16)

'Speak to one another with psalms, hymns and spiritual songs.' (Eph. 5:19)

'Greet one another.' (Rom. 16:16)

'Serve one another in love.' (Gal. 5:13)

God equips every believer to play a part in this mutual ministry. None of us can claim that we have nothing to offer. Paul insists that all believers have received spiritual gifts that are to be used for the common good.[14]

Grace gifts

The word Paul uses for 'spiritual gift' (*charisma*) has the word for grace (*charis*) as its root. Spiritual gifts are gifts of God's grace. *Charisma* has a broad usage in the New Testament. For example, it appears in Romans 6:23 to speak of the gift of salvation: ' ... the wages of sin is death, but the [free] gift [*charisma*] of God is eternal life in Christ Jesus'. Elsewhere the word is used more specifically to refer to the way in which God blesses his churches through the different abilities belonging to individual members.

The most extensive teaching concerning spiritual gifts is found in 1 Corinthians 12-14. There seems to have been a group in Corinth who were proud because of their exercise of certain gifts, in particular the gift of tongues, and who looked down on those who did not have those gifts as being less spiritual. Paul is horrified by that attitude. He stresses that all those who are able to say 'Jesus is Lord' are spiritual – in other words, all Christians (v. 1-3). 'We were all baptised by one Spirit into one body ... and we were all given the one Spirit to drink' (v. 13).

---

[14] 1 Cor. 12:7.

By likening a local church to a body, Paul is able to stress both our unity and our diversity: 'The body is a unit, though it is made up of many parts' (v. 12). Some at Corinth had forgotten that. They tried to produce spiritual clones who all had the same gift – tongues. But Paul stresses that God has deliberately given us different gifts to ensure the proper functioning of the body.

The priority of love

Our gifts have been given for the good of the body, not for us as individuals. How we need to remember that! So often we long for gifts for the wrong reasons. We want an 'up-front' gift to impress others and to boost our egos. Or perhaps we want a 'supernatural' gift – not so that we might serve others, but so that others will look up to us as 'spiritual'. At one time I longed for the gift of tongues. Part of my motivation was that I felt left out: all my friends claimed to speak in tongues. But perhaps the strongest reason for my longing was that I thought it would give me a sense of assurance. If I were able to speak in tongues, then I would really know that God was at work in my life. But I was completely wrong. Spiritual gifts are not given to boost assurance. They are for the service of others, so that together we might be built up as a body.

It is no coincidence that the two great chapters on spiritual gifts in the Bible are split by 1 Corinthians 13, which is all about love: 'If I speak in the tongues of men and of angels, but have not love, I am only a resounding gong or a clanging cymbal ...' Love, not self-interest and pride, should drive our attitude to spiritual gifts. We should be longing, not for the gifts that make us feel good about ourselves, but rather for those which best enable us to serve others. In the last verse of chapter 12 Paul writes: '... eagerly desire the greater gifts' (v. 31). He is speaking of those gifts that most edify others. Chapter 14 then applies the principle of the priority of love more specifically: 'Follow the way of love and eagerly desire spiritual gifts, especially the gift of prophecy' (1 Cor. 14:1). Prophecy is preferable to tongues, as we have seen earlier, because it is more edifying.

Great Variety

Ten spiritual gifts are mentioned in 1 Corinthians 12. There are other lists in the New Testament, all of which are different (Rom. 12:6-8; Eph. 4:11; 1 Pet. 4:10-11). They reveal a great variety of gifts. There is no clear distinction made between what we might call natural endowments and supernatural gifts. Some appear almost mundane: service, encouragement, leading, giving, showing mercy. Even marriage and singleness are referred to as gifts (1 Cor. 7:7). Others are more spectacular: miraculous powers and gifts of healing. It is not clear what some gifts actually were. Nobody can say for sure what Paul meant by a 'message of wisdom' or a 'message of knowledge' (1 Cor. 12: 8). There is no doubt that there are many other gifts that are not specifically described as such in the New Testament. For example, music and hospitality are never spoken of as spiritual gifts, but surely they are. God undoubtedly uses people with those abilities to minister his grace to others.

So Paul does not give us an exhaustive list of gifts in 1 Corinthians 12. Some people focus too much on the details as they read the chapter and try to work out which of the gifts they have. But if we are to understand these chapters correctly, we must remember that they are corrective. Paul did not sit in his study and write down everything that all Christians for all time could possibly want to know about the subject. Rather, he was responding to a particular problem at a particular time.

He presumably mentions some of the gifts listed because they were especially prevalent in Corinth at the time as subjects of controversy. We should focus on the principles he teaches, rather than the details, if we are to understand the message for today.

The gift of the bassoon

I once heard an analogy that helped to make that point. Suppose a church has many members who play the bassoon. They are proud about this and give the impression that all truly spiritual people should be bassoon players. They also think it is their right to exercise their gift when the church meets. They insist: 'God has given us our gift and we must use it.' The result is chaos: fifty people playing the bassoon at the same time. Paul writes to correct this abuse. He affirms the gift: 'I play the bassoon as much as any of you. It is a good gift to have. The church is helped to praise God when someone plays.' But then he criticizes them: 'We're meant to be different and not all have the same gifts. That way we function best. So please, could you limit yourselves to just two bassoonists on each Sunday? And could some of you look to serve in other ways? How about learning another instrument or helping with the coffee after church?'

What would be our reaction if we unearthed that letter after two thousand years? Would we panic about the fact that no one in our music group plays the bassoon and that therefore we can not be a spiritual church? That would be to miss the point. There are hundreds of different gifts (means by which God can edify a congregation through the ability of one member). No church can conceivably manifest all the possible gifts at any one time. Paul does not expect us to. The point he is making is not that a spiritual church will have bassoon players, but rather the principle that there is a great variety in the gifts God has given. And he wants us to use those different gifts in the loving service of others.

How can I serve?

Some Christians seem to be paralysed. Rather than serving others, they are waiting to discover what their gift is. The right question to ask is not so much 'What is my gift?' as 'How can I serve?' As soon as we see a possible area of service that we could fill, we should get moving. And, in so far as God uses that service for the good of the church, we are exercising a spiritual gift. We may not be very good at discerning which areas of service we should fill. Other Christians can often see our gifts better than we can, so we should seek advice.

Sometimes love demands that we do not use our gifts. 1 Corinthians 14 is largely a chapter about *not* using gifts. Those who speak in tongues are urged to keep quiet unless someone can interpret what they are saying, and the number of prophets contributing to the meeting is limited to two or three (v. 29). There are many gifts in each congregation. It is impossible for us all to exercise them at once. Much of the time, the way of love involves restraint. If a church already has five people who can play the piano, a sixth who joins might be better used if she looks to serve in some other area. She might be a better piano player than Sunday School teacher, but if the real need is for a teacher of the children she should help meet that need if possible.

God wants to involve all his people in the work of building up the church, and he has given us gifts to help us do the job. When we attend church meetings, we should think of ourselves not as consumers but as workers. We should pray not just that we will be blessed, but that God would use us to bless others.

A service station

We have seen that the prime direction of our meetings as Christians is not from us to God, but rather from God to us. The focus is the congregation and its encouragement or edification. He builds us up through his word, the sacraments, and the spiritual gifts of every member. Howard Marshall has written: 'In a real sense the church is "a service station" where Christians are "serviced" so that they may serve God better.'[15] We do not meet to worship God so much as to encourage one another that we might be equipped to worship God better with the whole of our lives. But that does not mean that there is no activity in our meetings directed from us to God. The New Testament also makes it clear that Christians praised God and prayed when they met.

B. From us to God

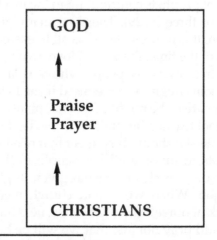

15 Marshall, *'How Far?'*, 227.

1. Praise

Although the New Testament does not describe Christian meetings as being for the purpose of worshipping God, it does tell us that elements within those meetings were addressed to God. One of the characteristic activities of the church after the day of Pentecost was 'praising God' (Acts 2:47). The Lord's Supper expressed thanksgiving to God (1 Cor. 10:16), as did songs (Eph. 5:19-20; Col. 3:16). We will return to the subject of music in the next chapter. Our whole lives should be an expression of gratitude to God, and we should certainly express that gratitude when we meet together.

2. Prayer

There are also many references in the New Testament to Christians praying when they met. On occasion they met specifically to pray, for example after the release of Peter and John (Acts 4:23-31). It is striking how often the early church is described as praying in the book of Acts.[16] In his sovereignty, God chooses to fulfil his purposes in answer to prayer. So it is vital that we pray. The importance of prayer should be reflected in the time we give to it in our main meetings and in the church's programme. There is no doubt that we miss out on much of God's blessing because we do not pray.

> O what grace we often forfeit,
> O what needless pain we bear;
> All because we do not carry
> Everything to God in prayer.[17]

---

[16] Acts 1:24; 6:6; 8:15; 12:12; 13:3; 14:23; 20:36; 21:5.
[17] From the hymn 'What a Friend We Have in Jesus' by J.M. Scriven (no. 746 in *Mission Praise* [Marshall Pickering, 1990]).

This movement from us to God is an important element in our meetings that should not be ignored. It can properly be described as worship. When we address God in praise and prayer in our meetings, we are worshipping him.

> A genuine relationship with God will involve ongoing expressions of submission to his character and will, in the form of personal and corporate acts of obedience, faith, hope and love. Prayer and praise should characterize Christian living in every context and must, therefore, be at the heart of any corporate engagement with God.[18]

But this is not the primary reason why we meet together.

Howard Marshall writes:

> When a specific function or purpose is ascribed to a church meeting it is not the glorification of God but the building up of the church and the ministry to its members. Church meetings are for the benefit of the congregation and so indirectly for the glory of God. Worship in the sense of giving praise to God is thus logically secondary to ministry in the sense of God's ministry to us.[19]

Marshall envisages a triangle that expresses the different movements that should take place in a Christian meeting.

The ministry of God's word to us is primary, for it equips all church members to engage in ministry to one another by the exercise of spiritual gifts. As we grow

---

[18] Peterson, *Engaging*, 195.
[19] Marshall, '*How Far?*', 227.

together in knowledge and love of God through Christ that, in turn, will lead to praise and prayer.

'Let us encourage one another'

Our survey of the Bible's teaching about Christian meetings should have convinced us that we need one another. It is vital that we meet together. Let us never delude ourselves into thinking that we can survive without other believers. God has not designed us to function on our own. We need other believers, and they need us.

So, when you go to church, remember that you are not just going to meet with God. You are also going to meet with other Christians. A friend of mine wrote these words to me after he had moved to a new area and was trying to settle into a church:

> On a whole number of occasions I have sat in an empty pew to be joined by a young family who not only fail completely to acknowledge my existence, but sit with their bodies angled away from me, facing entirely into

themselves. I end up wondering why they don't stay at home and watch 'Songs of Praise' on television.

That should not happen. We are not to be spectators when we go church; we are called to be active participants.

We should go to every church meeting thinking not just, 'What can I get out of it?' but also, 'How can I contribute?' Let us get into the habit of praying before we attend that God would use us in some way to encourage others. And then let us look out for opportunities to do that. Is there a newcomer we could welcome? A lonely person we could listen to? Someone who is discouraged whom we could urge on? We should not think that church begins with the opening song and ends with the last one. The time we have for interaction with one another before and after is just as important. It gives us an opportunity to get to know each other better. If possible, we should aim to arrive a little early and not rush off as soon as the formal part of the meeting is over. And we should look for other opportunities to build relationships – through meals or small groups, for example.

We are a family, and good families spend time with each other. The closer our relationships, the better we will be able to spur each other on in the Christian life. And the more we do that, the better we will worship God – not just on Sundays, but with the whole of our lives.

5

The Place of Music and Singing
'Sing and make music in your heart to the Lord'

From beginning to end, the Bible is full of music and song. The first musician, Jubal, makes his appearance as early as Genesis 4, where we are told that 'he was the father of all who play the harp and flute' (v. 21). As we turn the pages, we find many who follow in Jubal's musical footsteps. Moses sang a song of praise after the Exodus. Deborah sang after the victory over Sisera. King David played the harp and wrote many of the Psalms. The Lord Jesus sang a hymn with his disciples at the Last Supper. Paul and Silas sang a hymn of praise to God in jail. The book of Revelation tells us that there is plenty of singing in heaven as the heavenly choir joins in praise to God.[1]

The Bible makes it clear that we are not to wait until heaven. It contains frequent exhortations to us to sing. For example:

'Come, let us sing for joy to the Lord.' (Ps. 95:1)

---

[1] Ex. 15; Judg. 5; 1 Sam. 16:23; Mt. 26:30; Acts 16:25; Rev. 5:9.

'Sing to the Lord a new song, for he has done marvellous things.' (Ps. 98:1)

'Speak to one another with psalms, hymns and spiritual songs. Sing and make music in your heart to the Lord.' (Eph. 5:19)

The question we are addressing in this chapter is, 'Why?' Why does the Bible encourage us to sing and make music to the Lord? We are to sing in order to praise God and to encourage one another. We will examine this answer in more depth shortly. But first we will consider an answer that is often given today, but which has no basis in Scripture.

'Entering God's presence'

I received some publicity for a large Christian conference that urged me to attend with these words:

> Join us for dynamic teaching to set you on the right path, and inspiring worship where you can meet with God and receive the energy and love you need to be a mover and shaker in today's world. ... Alongside our teaching programme are worship events which put you in touch with the power and love of God.

Do you see the implication of what is said there? Bible teaching is good; it sets you on the right path. But it is through 'worship', by which they mean singing, that we meet with God and are put in touch with his love and power.

Some years ago I was on a mission in London. After one of our meetings, another team member came to me and said: 'Why don't you hold out your hands when you sing?' I have nothing against that practice. There are examples of it in the Bible. It can express something physically of what you feel in your heart. But I could not see why it seemed to matter so much to my friend. So I asked him: 'Why should I?' He replied: 'Because if you hold out your hands, you'll receive a blessing from God. He will come close to you and you'll feel his presence with you.'

He was expressing the view of many: we meet with God as we sing praise to him, especially when we do so in a particular way. The role of musicians and 'worship leaders' is to facilitate that encounter. These words were among the comments I read during a quick look at the backs of some Christian praise CDs:

> There are many kinds of music that enable us to enter the presence of God. We hope that this collection will bless you. We are committed to helping people world wide experience the manifest presence of God.

'The liver shiver'

Those musicians clearly equate 'entering God's presence' with a feeling. That conference publicity leaflet I mentioned earlier spoke of 'spine-tingling moments of worship'. A friend of mine refers to 'the liver shiver'. I guess we know what he means. No doubt there have been moments when we have felt our whole bodies tingling. Our emotions have been switched on, and it has been almost as if we have been transported out of ourselves.

We are all different, so different things induce the experience in us. Some find that dimly lit medieval buildings, candles, plainsong and formal choirs do it for them. Others are left cold by all that. Acoustic guitars, drums and synthesizers are what they need. Those two settings could hardly be more different, but many devotees of each are united by the belief that the 'buzz' they experience is an encounter with God. That buzz, in their minds, is the moment of true worship – when they enter the presence of God himself and he draws close to them.

If that is how they think, it is no wonder that they go to Christian meetings looking, above all, for an experience. They would not put it like that. They would say that they want to meet with God. But it is the same thing, since they equate meeting with God with a feeling. They are looking for a choir, group or band that will deliver the experience they want. If their spine tingles or their liver shivers, they go home satisfied. They have had a good 'time of worship'; they have met with God. But have they?

How do I know that my experience is a genuine encounter with the living God? Music has great power to generate emotion. No doubt you have been deeply moved at a concert or just listening to a favourite CD – Beethoven or the Beatles, Rimsky-Korsakov or Robbie Williams. But you did not call that an experience of God. How can you be sure that the feeling you had at that Christian meeting was God's presence with you rather than just the effect of some good music?

The Bible never teaches that a feeling can take us into the presence of God. If that had been possible, God would have sent us a musician rather than a saviour. Only Christ can take us into the Most Holy Place in heaven, where we have direct access to the Father through faith in him.

The very common view that 'worship' is essentially a time of singing through which we are drawn close to God has a number of harmful consequences.

The consequences of viewing music as an encounter with God

1. God's word is marginalized

In churches and Christian Unions all over the world, there is less and less time given to Bible teaching. Many people do not want to think. They just want to feel God's presence, and they look to music to give them that feeling. But we only encounter God through faith in Jesus, not through music. And how can we have faith in him unless we hear about him? Paul writes: 'faith comes from hearing the message, and the message is heard through the word of Christ' (Rom. 10:17).

What is more important to you: music or the Bible? When you choose a church, do you choose the one that has the best music group or the one that teaches the Bible best? Music is important, and I will have much more to say about that later. But it would be possible to survive in our faith without it. We could not survive, however, without God's word. It is by his word that God brings us into relationship with himself as we hear about Jesus and put our faith in him. It is also by his word that we are kept in our Christian faith as the living God addresses us with both challenges and encouragements.

Some respond by saying: 'That is fine; we do need the Bible. But we also need the Spirit. God speaks to our minds through his word, but he deals with our emotions through his Spirit.' That sort of response reveals a serious misunderstanding of the relationship between God's word and God's Spirit. The Bible never allows us to split the two. The Spirit of God is the divine author of the Bible and continues to speak through it today.[2] The

---

[2] 1 Cor. 2:13; 2 Tim. 3:16; 2 Pet. 1:21; Heb. 3:7; Rev. 2:7.

word of God is 'the sword of the Spirit'.[3] So, if we want
to be in close touch with the work of God the Spirit, it is
vital that we listen to his word.

2. *Our assurance is threatened*

If I associate the presence of God with an experience,
what happens when I no longer feel it? I am bound to
assume that I am no longer close to him. So I may suffer
a crisis of faith when I move from a church with a large
music group. My new church does teach the Bible, but
Mrs Jones' organ playing can never deliver the high that
I used to get in the last place.

But our assurance of God's love does not depend on
our feelings. Our assurance depends instead on the finished work of Christ. My feelings cannot take me any
closer to God – nor can they take me any further away
from him.   If I trust in Christ then I am already in God's
presence by faith, 'seated ... with him in the heavenly
realms in Christ Jesus' (Eph. 2:6). So I must look to him
alone if I want assurance – and not to my feelings, which
go up and down.

Charles Spurgeon once said: 'I looked at Christ, and
the dove of peace flew into my heart. I looked at the
dove, and it flew away.'

3. *Musicians are exalted*

Huge expectations are placed on musicians. They are
asked to play a priestly role and bring us into the presence of God by producing an experience. Churches are
increasingly appointing 'worship leaders' who bear the
weight of this expectation on their shoulders. If they fail

---

[3] Eph. 6:17.

to deliver, someone else soon replaces them. The most skilful discover what it is that works for their particular congregation. They know the songs, instruments and key changes that produce the desired effect. They are in great demand at conferences and conventions. Their names appear prominently in all the publicity.

There are dangers in all this. We can be too quick to give significant responsibilities to musicians. That young man may be a brilliant guitar player and have a dynamic, upfront manner, but how well does he know the Bible? Do the songs he chooses teach the truth clearly, or do they convey unbiblical emphases? Does he leave us with a sense of the wonder of Christ or just with a warm glow? The best Christian musicians will not primarily be seeking to produce an experience, which is easily manufactured once a few techniques are learned. They will, rather, be pointing to Christ and focusing attention on the truth about him.

4. Division is increased

If I identify an experience with a genuine encounter with God, and only a certain kind of music gives me that experience, then it will be very important to me that that kind of music is played regularly in my church or Christian Union. That will cause no problems if everyone shares my tastes. But if others feel they need different kinds of music, there is bound to be trouble. That explains why music is one of the greatest causes of division in Christian circles. There is very little tolerance. Particular music styles are associated with an authentic encounter with God. Those with other preferences are dismissed as unspiritual old fuddy-duddies or mindless, frothy youngsters.

But the style of music is in fact irrelevant. Of course we will have our preferences, but they are of no significance compared with the words that we sing. Truth is ultimately what matters, not tunes.

All I have said so far has been designed to warn against adopting too high a view of music. But we must not overreact and go to the opposite extreme. The Bible has a high regard for the place of singing in the Christian's life, and so should we. The Bible gives two reasons why we should sing. First, we should sing to praise God and, second, we should sing to encourage one another.

Why should we sing?

1. We should sing to praise God

Praise should be one of the characteristic activities of the Christian. The apostle Peter tells us:

... you are a chosen people, a royal priesthood, a holy nation, a people belonging to God, that you may declare the praises of him who called you out of darkness into his wonderful light (1 Pet. 2:9).

We have been called to belong to God for the purpose of declaring his praises.

Praise is natural

C.S. Lewis wrote:

All enjoyment spontaneously overflows into praise unless (sometimes if) shyness or the fear of boring others is deliberately brought in to check it. The world rings with praise – lovers praising their mistresses, readers their favourite poet, walkers praising the countryside.[4]

The Christian's praise of God should be just as natural. We should be so excited about who God is and what he has done for us that we want to tell others.

A stranger knocked on my door recently. I invited him in and he began to tell me his story. A number of years earlier, he had had an argument with his parents and left home. His life went downhill rapidly, and he ended up in Oxford in a terrible state. He was homeless, depressed and on drugs. 'I was in the gutter,' he said. But one day he knocked on the rectory door of St Ebbe's and spoke to one of my predecessors. He was pointed to the Lord Jesus and his life was turned upside down. He trusted in Christ for forgiveness and asked for his help to change. Within days he was back home and his recovery had begun. He finished: 'I am now a qualified barrister, I'm married and we're expecting our first child. I am still trusting Christ. I owe everything to him and I just wanted to tell someone.'

It was not difficult for that man to tell his story. If something wonderful has happened to us, we long to spread the news. It would be very strange if you kept news of a baby, a promotion or a good exam result entirely to yourself. And it would be strange if we never told others the wonderful news about a God who loved us so much that he sent his Son to die for us so that he could pick us out of the gutter. Whenever we do that, whether we are talking to a Christian or a non-Christian, we are praising him. But praise will also include speaking or singing to him directly.

---

[4] Quoted in David Watson *I Believe in the Church* (London: Hodder & Stoughton, 1982), 183.

When we praise God we are engaged in the activity that is most authentically human, for we are doing that for which we were created. We are made in God's image to reflect his majesty. God's goal in calling us to belong to him as Christians is that we might be 'for the praise of his glory'.[5] A friend of mine has said that: 'A song of praise is like a mirror we hold up to God, reflecting his glory back to himself'.[6]

Emotions and singing

If it is natural to praise, it is also natural to sing. James writes: 'Is any one of you in trouble? He should pray. Is anyone happy? Let him sing songs of praise' (Jas. 5:13). Singing is one of the ways in which we express our emotions. I said earlier that we should not equate emotions with the presence of God. I might get 'the liver shiver' when my side scores a goal at a football match or when I listen to some beautiful music at a concert, but I do not say: 'I've met with God.' We should not assume that we have encountered God just because we get emotional. It might simply have been the skill of the musicians or the beauty of the songs that moved us. But please do not conclude from that that we should be wary of all emotion.

We *should* be emotional about our faith. Those of us who come from the United Kingdom can be more British than biblical. We tend to be scared of showing any emotion. We can sing of the most wonderful truths with an expression on our faces that would be appropriate in a

---

[5] Eph. 1:6; 12, 14.
[6] Richard Simkin, in an excellent series of talks with David Jackman on 'Worship in Spirit and Truth', available from the Proclamation Trust Tape Ministry, 140-148 Borough High Street, London, SE1 1LB.

morgue. But why do we think God tells us to sing? Surely it is because singing enables us to express our emotions. It is not the means by which we enter the presence of God, but it is one of the ways in which we can express our joy at the wonderful truth that we are already there, in his presence, in Christ. Sometimes songs will help us to express the emotion that we already feel. On other occasions they will begin to trigger emotions, as the music helps us to feel something of the wonder of the truths we are singing about. The words 'ransomed, healed, restored, forgiven' might not move us especially when we see them written on a page, but they can come alive as we sing them and reflect on all that they describe.

God-focused songs

The fact that we sing to praise God should mean that our songs are focused on him, not us. There is certainly a place for telling him how we feel about him. There are plenty of examples of that in the Psalms. Some of them are intensely personal. Psalm 18 begins: 'I love you, O Lord, my strength', or Psalm 89: 'I will sing of the Lord's great love for ever'. But the Psalms of praise are never simply subjective declarations of the psalmists' feelings. The objective reasons for those feelings are always given, namely the greatness of God. For example: 'The Lord is my rock, my fortress and my deliverer' (Ps. 18:2), or: 'your love stands firm for ever ... you established your faithfulness in heaven itself' (Ps. 89:2).

Too many of our contemporary songs place an excessive emphasis on us – on how we feel about God and what we will do for him – and not enough emphasis on him. We can only express our love for him if we are first reminded of his love for us. That is where our focus must be: 'We love because he first loved us' (1 Jn. 4:19).

God-focused singing

The fact that we are addressing God as we sing should mean that we do so with reverence. That certainly does not rule out joy and fun. Those who object to children's songs with actions, for example, are surely going too far. But we should remember that, as someone has put it: 'We approach the almighty God, not the all-matey God.' He is our loving Father but he is also our awesome, holy creator. We should approach him with both love and 'reverent fear'.[7] We can be intimate, but not casual, confident, but not presumptuous. Those of us who lead the singing at Christian meetings should be careful with the words we use and the manner we adopt.

Reverence should also mean that we pay attention to the words we sing. It is so easy to switch into autopilot without letting the lyrics engage with our minds at all. God deserves better than that. John Wesley wrote in his 'Rules for Methodist Singers':

> Above all, sing spiritually. Have an eye to God in every word you sing. Aim at pleasing him more than yourself or any other creature. In order to do this, attend strictly to the sense of what you sing and see that your heart is not carried away with the sound, but offered to God continually.[8]

Musicians should seek to play, not to impress others, but to bring glory to God. Everything we do can be an

---

[7] 1 Pet. 1:17.
[8] Quoted in the Preface to *Christian Hymns* (Bryntirion: Evangelical Movement of Wales, 1977).

expression of praise. We can use all sorts of instruments for the purpose. Psalm 150 alone speaks of the trumpet, lute, harp, timbrel, strings, pipe and loud clashing cymbals. I take it that was a fairly representative sample of the instruments that were available at the time. Any kind of instrument can be used as a means of praising God.

2. We should sing to encourage one another

'Be filled with the Spirit. Speak to one another with psalms, hymns and spiritual songs' (Eph. 5:18-19).

Paul is not urging us to receive a one-off experience when he instructs us to 'be filled with the Spirit'. The verb he uses is in the present continuous tense. A better translation is: 'keep on being filled with the Spirit'. He follows that command with a string of participles, which are lost in our English translations, which spell out what it means in practice. The original reads like this: 'Keep on being filled with the Spirit, speaking to one another with psalms, hymns and spiritual songs; singing and making music in your heart to the Lord; always giving thanks to God the Father for everything, in the name of our Lord Jesus Christ; submitting to one another out of reverence for Christ' (vv. 18-21). It is striking that three of those five participles have to do with singing. Spirit-filled Christians sing.

'Speak' does not mean that we are only to read the words. Speaking includes singing as well. We tend to assume that we are to address our songs only to God, but Paul tells us that we are also to sing to 'one another'. We saw in the previous chapter that Christians in the New Testament met together primarily to encourage one another, and we are to do that even as we sing.

In Colossians Paul writes:

> *Let the word of Christ dwell in you richly as you teach and*
> *admonish one another with all wisdom, and as you sing*
> *psalms, hymns and spiritual songs with gratitude in your*
> *hearts to God.* (Col. 3:16)

Our singing should be one form of our ministry of God's
word to each other. We all need to be built up in our faith.
That happens through sermons, Bible studies, conversa-
tions – and also as we sing. Our songs should be one of
the ways by which we learn the truths of the Bible.

So, when we sing, we are not simply a collection of
individuals praising our God. We are a community
addressing one another. There are many examples of
that in the Psalms. Psalm 95, for example, is not so much
a song of praise to God as an exhortation to his people:
'Come, let us sing for joy to the Lord; let us shout aloud
to the Rock of our salvation' (v. 1). The Psalm then
strengthens that appeal by reminding us of reasons why
he is worthy of our praise: 'For the Lord is the great God,
the great King above all gods. In his hand are the depths
of the earth, and the mountain peaks belong to him'
(vv. 3-4).

The rehearsal of great truths about God simultane-
ously brings praise to him and encouragement to us.
Most songs, therefore, have two audiences: a heavenly
one and an earthly one. We should keep both the vertical and horizontal dimensions in mind as we choose
songs and as we sing them.

The power of music

Music has the power to embed words deeply into our
minds. Advertisers know that well. The Cadbury's jingle

from the 1970s is playing in my mind even as I write: 'Everyone's a fruit and nut case …' It is only marginally better than the more recent 'Magic Moments' tune.

The power of music is also evident in the Christian world. One Christian leader has said: 'I don't mind who writes the theological books so long as I can write the hymns.'[9] He was commenting on the great influence that our songs have on our theology. That can be harmful. The heretic Arius, who denied the divinity of Christ in the fourth century, used brief choruses with catchy tunes to spread his message. But if the words are good, the effect can be very positive.

I was greatly helped in the early months of my Christian life by the words of songs that I sang at a camp I attended soon after my conversion. Some were simply verses of Scripture put to music:

> My sheep hear my voice and I know them, and they fol-
> low me …

Others were distillations of biblical teaching:

> At the cross of Jesus, pardon is complete; love and justice
> mingle, truth and mercy meet. Though my sins condemn
> me, Jesus died instead; there is full forgiveness in the
> blood he shed.

Others were exhortations to live the Christian life:

> Be valiant, be strong, resist the powers of sin; the fight is
> long, the foe is strong, but you shall win; for through the
> power of Christ, the stronger than the strong, you shall
> be more than conqueror; be valiant, be strong.

---

[9] Quoted in Watson, *I Believe*, 192.

The tunes may sound dated now, but the words are still true. It is no exaggeration to say that I received as much biblical teaching and encouragement from those songs as from Bible studies and talks. My Christian understanding was largely formed by what I sang because those were the words that stuck with me. We must not underestimate the influence of the songs that we sing. One theologian said once: 'Show me your songs, and I will tell you your theology.' That means that great care must be taken in the choice of songs.

Choosing songs

If we want to ensure that our songs are edifying to others, we should consider four questions about them.

1. Are they true?

It is tempting simply to select the songs that are the most popular. But what do they teach? Are they faithful to Scripture? Is it really true that I can trade in my sorrows and sicknesses for the joy of the Lord, as one song I have been invited to sing suggests?[10] And will God give us all the ground we claim?[11]

We should not leave song writing to those who are gifted musically but who may not have much grasp of theology. The best of the classic hymns, like Charles Wesley's 'And can it be', are full of profound theology. There is an urgent need for more contemporary songs that follow in that tradition. They need not be long. One truth clearly stated can be enough. The Bible itself

---

[10] *Spring Harvest 2000*, no. 60.
[11] *Mission Praise*, no. 572.

should provide many of our lyrics. The Psalms are a rich resource that is not used nearly enough.

A learned academic from one of the colleges in Oxford came to St Ebbe's recently. He came up to me at the end of the meeting and pointed to some words on the song sheet and asked: 'Is that true? Can we sing it?' I was pleased that he asked that question. We should be concerned only to sing what is true. I was also pleased to be able to tell him that the words under suspicion came straight from Psalm 45.

2. Are they God-focused?

Our songs need to be focused on God – not simply so that we can praise him, but also so that we can be encouraged. If the majority of our songs are focused on ourselves, our feelings and our expressions of devotion to God, we will have little to sustain us through the rest of the week.

How have I been edified by singing:

> I will dance, I will sing, to be mad for my King; nothing, Lord is hindering the passion in my soul. And I'll become even more undignified than this; some would say it's fool-ishness, but I'll become even more undignified than this. And this. Na, na, na, na, na-hey (x7) Here I, here I, here I, here I go?[12]

There is a place for the subjective, but it should always be a response to the great objective truths about God.

Feelings come and go, but the truth never changes. It is the truth about God that drives my desire to keep worshipping him with all my life, even when that is difficult.

3. Are they clear?

Songs may be true and God-focused, but they will still not build anyone up unless they are also clear.

We slip into jargon so easily:

> We ride upon the breeze of your Spirit's lifting;

> I want to be out of my depth in your love.

And what does it mean that Jesus is:

> deeper than colour, richer than culture?[13]

Of course we should be able to use imagery and metaphor in our songs. Clarity does not demand dull expression. But the imagery should be such that it conveys the truth of which it speaks, rather than leaving us scratching our heads.

4. Are they unselfish?

Our songs should encourage us to sing to one another. If they are all in the first-person singular they will allow us to think only about ourselves and God. We could do that on our own. We should also direct our songs to those around us. It is gloriously true that as I 'behold the man upon a cross' I see 'my sin upon his shoulders'. That

---

[13] *Spring Harvest 2000*, no. 97; *Spring Harvest 1997*, nos. 63 and 79.

personal element has an important place in Christian songs. But it is also good to be reminded in the same song that God's love is for all God's people: 'How deep the Father's love for us'.[14]

Unselfishness should also influence our song selection in the sense that we should be thinking about what will most edify others, rather than about what we ourselves most want to sing. Love should be the controlling influence in our decisions about what we decide to include in our meetings.[15] It is a good sign if the older people in a fellowship are often saying: 'Let's have more modern songs for the youngsters,' and if the younger ones are saying: 'Let's have more hymns for the older folk.'

Singing and playing horizontally

If we grasp that one of the reasons why we sing is to build up others, we will make sure that we have them in mind. We will be aware of the horizontal dimension and not just the vertical. I should not sing: 'This is our God, the servant King, he calls us now to follow him'[16] with my eyes closed. I should be singing to you. And, whatever the words, I should sing with gusto. No one is encouraged by a dirge.

Those who play instruments should also have others in mind. Some musicians are more concerned about their performance than about serving others. We have all heard of choirs who have resigned because they have been restricted to one anthem a fortnight, or pianists who have

[14] *Spring Harvest 2000*, no. 45 (emphases mine).
[15] That point is made powerfully in 1 Cor. 13.
[16] *Mission Praise*, no. 162.

left churches because they are no longer allowed to choose the songs. There is an old joke circulating among ministers: 'What is the difference between an organist and a terrorist?' 'You can negotiate with a terrorist.'

Playing in church can be very hard for musicians. They often have to play music that they do not like or that is not very challenging for them. There may be songs that would give them a chance to show off their talents better, but that is not the object of the exercise. One of the world's most gifted organists was a member of our congregation until recently. You would not have known it. That is not because he did not play well, but rather because he resisted the temptation to perform.

'The noble art of music'

We have seen that some have too high a view of music and see it as a means by which we encounter God. Although the Bible does not teach that, it does assign an important role to singing. We are to sing to praise God and to encourage one another. Martin Luther once wrote: ' [After] the word of God, the noble art of music is the greatest treasure in the world'. [17]

---

[17] Quoted in *The Briefing* 252 (May 2001), 8.

6

Understanding the Lord's Supper
'Do this in remembrance of me'

It is a remarkable fact that the Lord's Supper, which is common, at least in essence, to almost all professing Christians, is a mystery to many. Most people believe that as they receive the bread and the wine they meet Christ in a special way, but few are able to explain why or how. The way the sacrament is served often seems designed to foster this sense of mystery. We often hide the simple rite that Jesus instituted beneath layer upon layer of religious packaging. The result is that many attend the Lord's Supper week after week and yet receive little, if any, true spiritual benefit. If we are to recover the sacrament as a means of grace, we must remove the packaging and return to the Bible's teaching on the subject. This teaching may be found in the three gospel accounts of the first Lord's Supper and in two passages in 1 Corinthians.

A. The first Lord's Supper

The Gospels point to three reasons why Jesus behaved as he did at the first Lord's Supper. The first Lord's

Supper[1] was an explanation of his death, an anticipation
of heaven and the institution of a memorial meal.

1. An explanation of his death

It is clear that Jesus intended his actions at the Last
Supper to be understood as an acted parable that
explained the meaning of the violent death that he knew
he was about to suffer. The bread and the wine symbol-
ize that violent death. They represent his broken body
and shed blood.

a) Passover

All of the Gospels stress that the Lord's Supper was a
Passover meal.[2] So, Jesus was doing what his forefathers
had done for centuries when, the night before he was
betrayed, he gathered with his disciples in the upper
room. But this was a Passover meal with a difference.

For generations, the head of the household had
picked up the unleavened bread and said: 'This is the
bread of the affliction that our fathers ate as they came
out of Egypt.' Jesus repeated the familiar action and
picked up the bread, but he used different words: 'This
is my body given for you.'[3] After the meal he took the
cup, another familiar feature of the Passover meal, and
said: 'This is my blood of the covenant.'[4]

The significance of these new words would not
have escaped the disciples' notice. Jesus was boldly

---

[1] Mt. 26:17-30; Mk. 14:12-26; Lk. 22:7-23.

[2] It is not clear whether it was eaten at the same time as the
festival or a little earlier, as suggested by the chronology of
John's Gospel.

[3] Lk. 22:19.

[4] Mt. 26:28.

reinterpreting the whole Passover festival. It finds its fulfilment in him: he is 'the Lamb of God, who takes away the sin of the world' (Jn. 1:29). The Passover lambs died instead of the Israelite firstborn sons so that the sons might escape God's judgement. Jesus' death is also a substitutionary sacrifice, which rescues his people from the judgement of God.

b) New covenant

A covenant is a formal binding agreement. It was customary in ancient times for such agreements to be ratified in blood. For example, God's covenant with Moses was ratified through sacrifices. We are told in Exodus 24 that: 'Moses then took the blood, sprinkled it on the people and said, "This is the blood of the covenant that the Lord has made with you"' (Ex. 24:8). The people of Israel broke that covenant, but Jeremiah prophesied a new and lasting covenant. God spoke through him and said:

> 'The time is coming,' declares the lord, 'when I will make a new covenant with the house of Israel and with the house of Judah. It will not be like the covenant I made with their forefathers when I took them by the hand to lead them out of Egypt, because they broke my covenant, though I was a husband to them,' declares the LORD. 'This is the covenant that I will make with the house of Israel after that time,' declares the LORD. 'I will put my law in their minds and write it on their hearts. I will be their God, and they will be my people. No longer will a man teach his neighbour, or a man his brother, saying, "Know the LORD," because they will all know me, from the least of them to the greatest,' declares the LORD. (Jer. 31:31–34)

God promised a whole new basis on which he would relate to his people. They would have a desire to obey him deep within their hearts, a true knowledge of himself and they would know that he had forgiven their sins. That was the new covenant. But something was missing. The covenant had not been ratified. That required blood, for 'without the shedding of blood there is no forgiveness' (Heb. 9:22). It is in this context that the words of Jesus as he took the cup find their significance. He said: 'This is my blood of the covenant, which is poured out for many for the forgiveness of sins' (Mt. 26:28). He is pointing to his death as the ratification of the new covenant. Its promises now become reality for his people.

c) Personal application

In calling on his disciples to eat and drink his body and blood Jesus was stressing the need for personal appropriation of the blessing that would be achieved by his death. The Israelites in Egypt only benefited from the sacrifice of the Passover lamb once its blood had been sprinkled on their doors, thus signifying that the household within trusted in the effects of its death. Jesus' actions at the Last Supper made it clear that his death demanded a similar response if it was to be effective for individuals. He had already taught this truth explicitly when he said:

> *I tell you the truth, unless you can eat the flesh of the Son of Man and drink his blood, you have no life in you. Whoever eats my flesh and drinks my blood has eternal life, and I will raise him up at the last day.* (Jn. 6:53-54)

These words in their context do not refer primarily to the Lord's Supper. They simply state the same truth that is visibly expressed at that supper. Jesus is not speaking literally. There is no support here for the doctrine of transubstantiation. In John 6, as in the institution of the Last Supper, Jesus is teaching in a very vivid and powerful way that the benefits of his death are not received automatically. They must be received by faith. In a clear parallel with verse 54, Jesus says: 'everyone who looks to the Son and believes in him shall have eternal life, and I will raise him up at the last day' (v 40).

2. An anticipation of heaven

The Jews often spoke of the great blessings of the Messianic age in terms of a banquet. Jesus himself used this language to speak of what would happen at the end of time.[5] At the Last Supper he pointed his disciples to that great moment when he said: 'I tell you, I will not drink of this fruit of the vine from now on until that day when I drink it anew with you in my Father's kingdom' (Mt. 26:29). The Last Supper, with the Messiah and his people eating together, is thus an anticipation of the great banquet which will be enjoyed when God's kingdom comes in all its fullness. Jesus is filling his disciples with hope to sustain them through the hard times ahead.

3. The institution of a memorial meal

Jesus intended to set a pattern at the Last Supper that was to be repeated. He said: 'do this in remembrance of me' (Lk. 22:19). The early Christians did as he commanded. When Paul introduces the subject of the 'Communion' in 1 Corinthians 10:16 he clearly presupposes that it is a familiar action. Passages in Acts suggest

---

[5] E.g., Mt. 22:1-14.

that it may have been celebrated weekly or even daily.[6] This regular celebration has continued through the centuries but, sadly, the Eucharistic rite of the church has often strayed a long way from the simple supper instituted by its founder. Keeping in mind these biblical foundations for Jesus' institution of this meal, we now need to look further at the Bible's teaching to discover the way in which Jesus intended this lasting ceremony to be celebrated.

B. The Lord's Supper today

Two significant passages in 1 Corinthians, 10:14-22 and 11:17-34, reveal Paul's understanding of the Lord's Supper. They point us to four elements that should be present in any celebration of the meal today.

1. Remembrance

The church at Corinth had been behaving badly when they met to share the bread and the wine. Paul goes so far as to tell them: 'your meetings do more harm than good' (1 Cor. 11:17). In chapter 11 he seeks to remind them of how the meal should be eaten by speaking of its institution. He quotes the words of Jesus after he had broken the bread: 'This is my body, which is for you; do this in remembrance of me' (v. 24). He goes on to say that the act of eating the bread and drinking the wine is a 'proclamation' of the Lord's death (v. 26). The Lord's Supper is meant to anchor the church to the event which lead to its creation: the cross of Christ, 'lest we forget'.

---

[6] Acts 2:42, 46.

That focus, unfortunately, is often blurred. This is found, for example, in changes in the liturgy of the Church of England. The old *Book of Common Prayer* (BCP) communion service focuses exclusively on the cross. It states that we receive the bread and the wine 'in remembrance of [Christ's] death and passion'. A number of the new orders for Holy Communion in *Common Worship*, following the lead of the previous *Alternative Services Book*, confuse the issue by encouraging us to remember much else besides. Eucharistic Prayer B is typical:

> And so Father, calling to mind his death on the cross, his perfect sacrifice made once for the sins of the whole world; rejoicing in his mighty resurrection and glorious ascension, and looking for his coming in glory, we celebrate this memorial of our redemption.[7]

The result is that the unique focus on the cross is lost.

It is not just unclear liturgy that can draw attention away from the cross. The average non-Christian (and, sadly, many Christians too) would assume from the way many churches conduct the Lord's Supper that the focus of the action is on the present. That was certainly the impression I received before my conversion. I noticed that all the important action was taking place in what seemed to be a special part of the building behind a rail, which kept most people out. Only special people entered, wearing special clothes and gathered around an elaborately adorned special table. Clearly those involved considered that something very important was happening, but I was left baffled as to what it was.

---

[7] *Common Worship* (London: Church House Publishing, 2000), 190.

All that ritual served to focus my attention on the present, while preventing me from seeing beyond the present to the past, to which it should have pointed. I was left with a vague belief that somehow the 'priest' was making God specially present on the 'altar' in a way that he had not been before. I therefore assumed that I got closer to God at a communion service than at any other time.

Sometimes I felt close to him. The ancient building, beautiful singing and ornate ritual all combined to give me a warm glowing feeling which I identified as the presence of God. That is the equivalent of the 'liver-shiver theology' that we considered in Chapter 5 in connection with music. But it is Christ, not an experience, who brings us close to God. Unless the Lord's Supper points us to Christ and his cross, and thus to the gospel, it cannot in fact draw us closer to God – whether it leads to us feeling closer to him or not.

Much of the current popularity of the Lord's Supper is based on mysticism (the feelings it induces) rather than on the fact that it reminds us of the gospel. Of course attendance at communion can be profoundly moving. The difference between a mystic and a truly Christian experience of communion is that the mystic has the experience directly. The Christian's heart and emotions, on the other hand, are affected indirectly, via the mind, as his or her attention is focused in a visible, tangible way on the wonder of the gospel of the cross. Unless the mind has been directed back in remembrance to the cross, no true Lord's Supper has taken place.

2. *Communion*

Remembrance is at the heart of any true celebration of the Lord's Supper, but that is not the end of the matter.

While our attention must primarily be focused on the past, something significant is also happening in the present. Paul's questions in 1 Corinthians 10 point us to that present reality:

> Is not the cup of thanksgiving for which we give thanks a participation in the blood of Christ? And is not the bread that we break a participation in the body of Christ? (v. 16)

As we receive the bread and the wine we may have 'communion' or 'participation' with Christ. John Stott has commented:

> Jesus did not only break the bread; he gave it to the disciples to eat. He did not only pour out the wine; he gave it to them to drink. ... He was not content that they should watch and listen; they must eat and drink. So the service is a communion as well as a commemoration.[8]

That much is straightforward, but to go further is to enter a battleground. How is it that we participate in the body and blood of Christ in the Lord's Supper? More ink and blood have been spilt over the answer to that question than over any other in church history. Much depends on how one understands the words of Jesus: 'this is my body', 'this is my blood'.

The Roman Catholic Church has taken the words literally. Its official teaching is often called 'transubstantiation', expressed as follows at the Council of Trent:

> By the consecration of the bread and the wine there takes place a change of the whole substance of the bread into

---

[8] John Stott, *Your Confirmation* (London: Hodder & Stoughton, 1958), 99.

the substance of the body of Christ our Lord and of the
whole substance of the wine into the substance of his
blood.[9]

This change is believed to occur as the words of institution ('This is my body', etc.) are repeated by the
priest. There is a more detailed look at Roman
Catholic understandings of the Lord's Supper in the
Appendix.

The Orthodox Churches in the East also believe in
transubstantiation. They believe this is effected by the
Holy Spirit as the celebrant prays that by the power of
the Spirit the elements may become Christ's body and
blood. That prayer is known as the *epiclesis*. That literal
understanding of the elements as the very body
and blood of Christ, shared by both the Orthodox and
Roman Catholic churches, leads to the view that communion occurs simply when they are eaten and drunk.
Thus the sacrament achieves spiritual good automatically (*ex opere operato*). The recipients receive Christ as
they take the elements, whether or not they appreciate
what is happening.

This doctrine of transubstantiation cannot be sup-
ported by the clear teaching of Scripture. Surely the
apostles did not understand Jesus, standing before them
in the flesh, to mean that the bread and wine before him
had actually become his body and blood. He was speaking symbolically. A soccer manager, while describing a
planned move over a meal before the game, might pick
up a salt cellar and say: 'This is the goalkeeper.' No one
thinks he is speaking literally. Nor is Jesus. He is saying:
'This represents my body'.

---

[9] Quoted in *Catechism of the Catholic Church* (London:
Geoffrey Chapman, 1994), 310.

Jesus is referring not to his body present before them, nor to his resurrected body, but rather to his crucified body. John Stott again puts it clearly:

> The communion bread is broken; it stands for the body of Jesus not as it lived in Galilee or Judea, but as it was broken or given in death on the cross. The wine is poured out; it stands for the blood of Jesus not as it flowed in His veins while He lived, but as it was shed on the cross. So the body and blood of Christ signify not Christ's life, but His death.[10]

Old Testament references to 'eating a man's flesh' or 'drinking his blood', which speak of enjoying the benefits that might result from someone's death, also support this understanding.[11]

It is clear, therefore, that the bread and wine remain bread and wine no matter what words or prayers are said over them. It is possible to receive them and not receive the body and blood of Christ. However, as words are said which give the elements significance, pointing to the death of Christ, those elements become a visible word, preaching the gospel. They speak of the cross and of the forgiveness that is offered as a result of it. Believers recognize the gospel in these symbols and respond with faith. The act of eating and drinking for them is thus more than merely physical. In their hearts they are eating and drinking the body and blood of Christ – finding spiritual nourishment again in the gospel. As Charles Spurgeon wrote: 'We not only eat of

---

[10] Stott, *Your Confirmation*, 99.

[11] Psalm 14:4; 27:2; 2 Sam. 23:15-17 (A.M. Stibs, *Sacrament, Sacrifice and Eucharist* [London: Tyndale Press, 1961], 51.

his bread, but symbolically we feast upon him.'[12] There is a 'real presence' of Christ at the Lord's Supper, but it is located in the heart of the believer, not in the elements themselves. Communion occurs by faith. As Article 28 of the Church of England puts it:

> The body of Christ is given, taken, and eaten in the Supper only after a heavenly and spiritual manner. And the means whereby the Body of Christ is received and eaten in the Supper is faith.

So, true communion does occur at the Lord's Supper. It depends on remembrance. As we remember the death of Christ, through the symbols of bread and wine, we are called to receive the benefits of that death by faith, which is symbolized by the act of eating and drinking.

3. Fellowship

This remembrance and communion is something we should do together. Paul speaks of 'participation' in the body and blood of Christ (1 Cor. 10:16). The Greek word he uses is *koinonia*, or 'fellowship'. We should not speak of 'making *my* communion' as if it is an entirely private matter between me and him. The word Paul uses stresses that we participate in the body and blood of Christ *together*.

In 1 Corinthians 11 he uses the verb 'to come together' five times in 18 verses in the context of the Lord's Supper. Our common participation in the meal is a sign of our unity. Each receives from the same

---

[12] Quoted in E.F. Kevan, *The Lord's Supper* (Darlington: Evangelical Press, 1966), 22.

loaf because each belongs to the same body. 'Because there is one loaf, we, who are many, are one body, for we all partake of the one loaf' (1 Cor. 10:17). 'The loaf is an emblem of the crucified Saviour, and it is our common participation in him (symbolized by our common participation in it) which makes us one'.[13] The Lord's Supper is a meal which should express our fellowship not just with Christ, the unseen head of the table, but also with the others who share in the same food.

This corporate element is too often obscured by the way in which we administer the bread and wine. We sit in a row, avoiding eye contact, as we each take our own individual tiny piece of bread or wafer; or we join a queue and kneel at the rail, facing straight ahead, heads bowed in prayer. The 'sharing of the peace' may pay lip-service to the fact that others are present, but it rarely produces real engagement with them. It is fundamentally different from the original setting of the Lord's Supper.

The first Christians took bread and wine in the context of a fellowship meal. We would gain much if we followed their example. A meal is an ideal context in which to take the bread and wine in remembrance of Christ. We at St Ebbe's have recently started a tradition of having a 'Church Family Meal' in the week before Easter. We enjoy eating together and getting to know each other better. At some time during the meal we pause to think briefly about Christ's death for us and then share bread and wine. It is one of the highlights in our church's calendar. We try to provide other similar opportunities, although not enough. A fellowship group in a home can be another good setting in which to share the Lord's

---

[13] Stott, *Your Confirmation*, 102.

Supper. There is no biblical reason why an ordained person should preside.[14]

Of course it is not always practicable to administer the bread and wine during a meal. It is entirely appropriate to do so in one of our normal Sunday meetings, but we should do all we can in that setting to stress that it is something we do together. Fellowship is an important element in the Lord's Supper.

4. Hope

As we have already seen, Jesus anticipated heaven at the Last Supper. Paul maintained this future perspective when he said: 'whenever you eat this bread and drink this cup, you proclaim the Lord's death *until he comes*' (1 Cor. 11:26). Every time we celebrate the Lord's Supper we are experiencing a foretaste of heaven: gathering together as God's people to celebrate Christ's death. Both the heavenly and communal elements of the Lord's Supper are most powerfully expressed over a meal. It requires a great deal of imagination to picture a heavenly banquet when taking just a morsel of bread and a sip of wine.

Conclusion

The Lord's gift of his supper to Christians has been greatly abused over the years. On the one hand, some

---

[14] Catholic teaching insists that ordained priests are essential if true communion is to occur at the Lord's Supper because only they are able to make Christ present in the bread and wine. While Protestant denominations reject this teaching, most still require the Lord's Supper to be administered by an ordained minister to ensure that everything is done decently and in order, but there is no biblical reason that requires this limitation.

have overemphasized it as the predominant means of grace. Others have virtually neglected it. A biblical understanding should guard against both extremes. The New Testament makes it clear that we could receive the same blessing as we receive at the Lord's Supper through hearing God's word. 'It is a special means of grace but it is not a means of special grace.'[15] We do not receive anything at the Lord's Supper that we cannot receive elsewhere. The fact remains, however, that it is a wonderful means of grace. As together we receive the bread and wine, we are reminded of Christ's death, strengthened as we receive its benefits by faith, and encouraged by the prospect of heaven. How can we neglect a meal that offers us so much, and more?

It has been helpfully suggested that we should look in four directions if we are to make the most of this supper. Each summarizes one of the points we have been considering.

1. Look back (remembrance)

I do not stop when I see a signpost to London. Its purpose is to point me away from itself to the city. But many stop at the bread and the wine instead of looking to Calvary, the place to which they point. We are to focus on the past, the moment when Jesus died.

2. Look up (communion)

As we look back, we are also to look up to Christ on whom we feed 'in our hearts by faith with

---

[15] Kevan, *Lord's Supper*, 23.

thanksgiving'.[16] The bread and wine provide us once more with an opportunity to trust in Christ's death for our salvation and to delight in him.

3. Look around (fellowship)

We should be conscious that we enjoy this meal with others, united together in Christ as one body.

4. Look forward (hope)

What we do at the Lord's Supper is a foretaste of heaven. When we finally get there, we will be gathered together with all of God's people, enjoying perfect communion with him and praising him for Christ's death on the cross which made that possible.

True worship

The prime direction of the Lord's Supper is from God to us, as he invites us to receive by faith the benefits of Christ's death. All true worship begins in the same way: with the perfect worship of the Lord Jesus, who offered his body as a sacrifice for us. It is his death alone that makes it possible for us to be acceptable worshippers in God's sight. And it does the job perfectly. We now have complete access to God through Christ. The only appropriate response is to offer our worship to God, our Creator, Redeemer and Father. That will include praising him in song, but it must go further than that. True worship is the offering to God of all that we have and

---

[16] The words of distribution in the *Book of Common Prayer* communion service.

are, in grateful response to Christ's offering of himself for us.

In the light of all that he has done for us, we should gladly echo the prayer Archbishop Cranmer placed at the end of his communion service in the *Book of Common Prayer*:

> And here we offer and present unto thee, O Lord, our-selves, our souls and bodies, to be a reasonable, holy, and lively sacrifice unto thee ... And although we be unworthy, through our manifold sins, to offer unto thee any sacrifice, yet we beseech thee to accept this our bounden duty and service; not weighing our merits, but pardoning our offences, through Jesus Christ our Lord; By whom, and with whom, in the unity of the Holy Ghost, all honour and glory be unto thee, O Father Almighty, world without end. Amen.

Appendix

Christ's Sacrifice and Ours

The major difference between Catholic and Protestant understandings of the Lord's Supper focuses on the issue of sacrifice. To what extent can we describe what is happening as a sacrifice? Protestants stress that the sacrifice of which the rite speaks took place and was finished when Jesus died. Catholics argue that in some sense there is a continuing sacrifice offered at the Eucharist.

This issue relates to our theme of worship and to issues that we have considered in previous chapters. Protestants stress that the prime direction of the action at the Lord's Supper is from God to us, as he symbolically offers the benefits of the completed sacrifice of Christ to believers. Catholics argue that the movement is from us to God, as the church offers a sacrifice to him.

There are a variety of ways in which Catholics (whether Roman, Anglican or Orthodox) understand this sacrifice. The traditional view is that the priest offers the body and blood of Christ on the altar at the 'Mass' as a propitiatory sacrifice that appeases God's wrath. This view was affirmed in the strongest terms by the Council of Trent at the time of the Counter-Reformation:

> The victim is one and the same, the same now offers
> through the ministry of priests who then offered himself
> on the cross; only the manner of offering is different. ...
> In this divine sacrifice which is celebrated in the Mass,
> the same Christ who offered himself once in a bloody
> manner on the altar of the cross is contained and is
> offered in an unbloody manner.[1]

Many still hold such understandings of the sacrifice of
the mass today, but there have also been new develop-
ments. Chief among these is the view that, at the
Eucharist, Christ's body, the church, enters into his continuing sacrifice of himself. The rite is seen, therefore,
not so much as a repetition of the sacrifice of the cross,
as previously taught, but as a perpetuation of it. This
view enables Catholics to affirm the biblical teaching
that the sacrifice of Christ was 'once for all', while still
speaking of the Eucharist as a sacrifice. For example, the
Second Vatican Council (1962–65) stated that the priests
're-present and apply in the sacrifice of the mass the one
sacrifice of the New Testament, namely the sacrifice of
Christ offering himself once for all to his Father as a
spotless victim'.[2]

References to a 'once for all' sacrifice of Christ appeal
to Protestant sensibilities and lead some to believe that
the differences between Catholic and Protestant
Eucharistic doctrine are now little more than a matter of
semantics. Closer inspection leads us to be less opti-
mistic. Our first objection must be that it is wrong to
think of Christ's one sacrifice being offered continually.
As we saw in Chapter 3, the New Testament clearly

---

[1] Quoted from the *Catechism of the Catholic Church*, 307.
[2] Quoted in John Stott, *The Cross of Christ* (Leicester: IVP, 1986), 226.

states that his sacrificial work was finished on the cross. Unlike the priests of the Old Testament, who had to stand day after day to offer their endless sacrifices, Christ was able to sit down after the cross, signifying that his work was done (Heb. 10:11-12). He does not continue to offer himself for our sins in heaven.

Our second objection to the new thinking concerns the idea that, as Christ's body, the church enters into his continuing sacrifice at the Eucharist. A.G. Herbert is one among many who has expressed this view:

> The sacrificial action is not any sort of re-immolation of Christ, nor a sacrifice additional to his one sacrifice, but a participation in it. The true celebrant is Christ, the High Priest, and the Christian people are assembled as members of his body to present before God his sacrifice, and to be themselves offered up in sacrifice through their union with him.[3]

The Agreed Statement of the Anglican Roman Catholic International Commission (ARCIC) says something similar: 'We enter into the movement of Christ's self-offering.'[4]

Once more we must say that the New Testament offers no support for this. Christ was uniquely able to offer himself for the sins of the world on the cross. Our sin disqualifies us from being involved in that sacrifice. We are the problem and cannot therefore participate in the solution, except as guilty sinners receiving the gift of forgiveness. Our role is passive, not active. Only once we have received forgiveness as a result of the sacrifice of Christ are we able to offer our own sacrifice: our lives

---

[3] Quoted from Stibbs, *Sacrament, Sacrifice*, 22.

[4] Quoted from Stott, *The Cross*, 269.

given over to his service. These two sacrifices, Christ's and ours, are radically different and should never be confused.

One of the major weaknesses of most of the new communion services in the Church of England is that they do confuse these sacrifices. Cranmer's liturgy in the *Book of Common Prayer* is at pains to divide them. All the emphasis is placed on Christ's 'full, perfect and sufficient sacrifice' until after the bread and wine are received. Only then is mention made of 'our sacrifice of praise and thanksgiving' and the offering of 'our souls and bodies to be a reasonable, holy, and lively sacrifice unto thee'. These sacrifices are in response to Christ's sacrifice on the cross, which we have just remembered.

But the newer Anglican liturgies confuse them by introducing words between the words of institution and the reception of the bread and the wine. Prayer F in *Common Worship*, for example, includes a prayer that the bread and the wine might 'form us into the likeness of Christ and make us a perfect offering in your sight'.[5] The result is to draw attention away from Christ's sacrifice and confuse it with ours. The Lord's Supper is also referred to as a 'memorial' – a word which suggests, to those who wish, that Christ's redemptive sacrifice is made present and effective in the service of communion, through which the church enters into his sacrifice.

This view that the Eucharist is a sacrifice offered by the church remains popular. Its supporters regard the officiant as a 'priest' who offers Christ at the altar, or who leads the people in their joint offering with Christ. The New Testament knows nothing of this. As Michael Green has commented:

---

[5] *Common Worship*, 1999.

> We do not come to offer; in the first place we come to
> receive. The very nature of a supper declares this. We are
> the hungry coming to be fed. We are the undeserving,
> welcomed freely at the Lord's table.[6]

Notice that it is the Lord who feeds us. The role of the
minister is that of a waiter, pointing us to him and to the
food he offers through his death. There is no biblical reason why this officiant should always be male, 'ordained'
or dressed in special clothes. The crucial participant at
the meal is its unseen host. It is his sacrifice we come to
remember and in which we find nourishment.

---

[6] Quoted from Stott, *The Cross*, 273.

Battles Christians Face

Tackling Big Issues with Confidence

Vaughan Roberts

The Bible is clear that the Christian's hope and faith are forged in the fiery battles of life. Suffering and temptation shape and strengthen us. But in the twenty-first century many of the crucial difficulties that Christians have always struggled with are lightly treated by some:

- How can I approach feelings of lust in a godly way when 'lust' is now an alluring name for perfume or chocolate?
- How can I battle guilt with integrity when friends encourage me to believe that sin doesn't really exist?
- Why do I feel so depressed when the impression is often given that Christians should always have a smile on their face and in their heart?

In *Battles Christians Face* Vaughan Roberts equips us with practical weapons to face our daily battles with confidence. The teaching in this book restores our hope of living godly lives here and now.

978-1-78078-115-0

Distinctives

Dare To Be Different

Vaughan Roberts

In fresh and readable style Vaughan Roberts issues a challenging call to Christians to live out their faith. We should be different from the world around us – Christian distinctives should set us apart in how we live, think, act and speak.

Targeting difficult but crucial areas such as our attitude to money and possessions, sexuality, contentment, relativism and service, this is holiness in the tradition of J.C. Ryle for the contemporary generation. Roberts helps us to consider how we are to respond biblically to the temptations and pitfalls surrounding us – giving what we cannot keep to gain what we cannot lose.

Will you take up the challenge?
Will you dare to be different?

978-1-85078-331-2

Turning Points

Vaughan Roberts

Is there meaning to life? – Is human history a random
process going nowhere? – Or is it under control, heading
towards a goal, a destination? – And what about my life?
Where do I fit in to the grand scheme of things?

These are topical questions in any age, but perhaps particularly so in a largely disillusioned postmodern era such as ours.
Vaughan Roberts addresses these questions and others as he
looks at what the Bible presents as the 'turning points' in history, from creation to the end of the world. This book does not
read like a normal history book. No mention is made of great
battles and emperors of whom we learnt at school. It will not
help you pass exams or score extra marks in a pub quiz. It aims
to do something far more important, to help you see history as
God sees it, so that you might fit in with his plans for the world.

978-1-85078-336-7

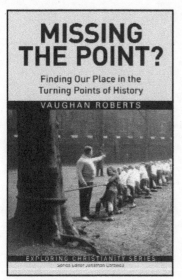

Exploring Christianity

Missing the Point?

Finding Our Place in the Turning Points of History

Vaughan Roberts

Is there a meaning to life? Where are we going? What is the purpose of it all?

Christians believe that the answers to all these questions are found in the Bible. It is an ancient book but it is also God's message to us today – a message that focuses on one man, Jesus of Nazareth.

Missing the Point? looks at the most important turning points of history as outlined in the Bible and considers where we have come from, where we are going and what this life is all about.

The *Exploring Christianity* series looks at some of the big issues in life, tackles them head on and leads you to the incomparable person of Jesus.

978-1-85078-763-1